Real Divas Win ™ Volume #1

REAL DIVAS WIN

"STORIES OF FAITH, VICTORY & SACRIFICE"

TIFFANY A. GREEN

REAL DIVAS WIN VOLUME #1
@Copyright 2018 by Tiffany A. Green
All rights reserved. No part of this book maybe reproduced or transmitted in any form or by any means without prior written permission from the author.
ISBN: 978-1-953638-05-2
Printed in the United States of America
This book or parts thereof may not be reproduced in any form, stored in a retrieval system, or transmitted in any form by any means-electronic, mechanical, photocopy, recording, or otherwise-without prior written permission of the publisher, except as provided by United States of America copyright law.

**PUBLISHER
TA MEDIA & PRODUCTIONS LLC
DALLAS, TX 75240
www.PUBLISHYOURBOOKTODAY.INFO
WWW.TAMEDIACO.COM**

Unless otherwise noted, all Scripture quotations are taken from the Holy Bible, King James Version (PUBLIC DOMAIN PER BIBLEGATEWAY.COM)

Holy Bible, New International Version®, NIV® Copyright ©1973, 1978, 1984, 2011 by Biblica, Inc.® Used by permission. All rights reserved worldwide.

The Holy Bible, English Standard Version. ESV® Text Edition: 2016. Copyright © 2001 by Crossway Bibles, a publishing ministry of Good News Publishers

DEDICATION

This book is dedicated to the many woman who have vowed to release their own stories to save thousands and millions of lives. This book was birthed not only to save lives but to also stand as an act of therapy and mental medicine. As we know, many women who experience the worst things in life are many times silenced and are threatened or too frightened to release what they've lived through. This then causes sickness, crucial mental illness, death and many other life issues that are untold. Women don't have to suffer; they can release through this platform and many others. The writers of the Real Divas Win Anthology are here for you and praying for your healing.

The sole mission of Real Divas Win is to comfort and allow a place for healing through writing to release, so that thousands of lives may be saved. It is our prayer that each and every word and chapter bless your life. May God Bless and Keep you

FOREWORD

Tiffany A. Green is a Christ centered, powerful, amazing, beautiful woman of God. Knowing her story, it is only fitting for Tiffany to be the leading force of "Real Divas Win."

I've had the opportunity to watch Tiffany's journey from adversity to greatness from a teenage mom, single mom, married woman, widow, motherless daughter and now soon to be First Lady. Praise God! Through each of these adversities she has shown strength, endurance and peace while walking in the favor and grace God has set before her.

Tiffany's giving spirit, the ability to empower, uplift, encourage and assist others epitomizes the essence of this title; she truly is a Real Diva that is Winning!

Many times, you think that God is thinking of you but HE is thinking about those you are going to assist, free, love, heal, restore and bring wholeness.

But you are a chosen people, a royal priesthood, a holy nation, God's special possession, that you may declare the praises of him who called you out of darkness into his wonderful light. 1 Peter 2:9

Tiffany, Sheila, Sasha, Jill, Marcie, Erica, Renee, Shequita, Alecia, TonShay, Toni, Leslie, Shonda, and April thank you for sharing your testimonies and I pray this book ministers to many as it go forth and do as God instructs it to do.

May God bless each of you for your gift of love and contribution of sharing your testimony to sow into others.

> Give, and it will be given to you. A good measure, pressed down, shaken together and running over, will be poured into your lap. For with the measure you use, it will be measured to you." Luke 6:38

Mitzi L. Carrasquillo~

Childhood Sexual Trauma Recovery Coach, Speaker and Author of "In Jesus Name, Please Don't Touch Me There" and the "Loved, Healed and Restored Daily Journal"

www.lovedhealedandrestored.com

Real Divas Win ™ Volume #1

TABLE OF CONTENTS

1. TIFFANY A. GREEN **10**
2. SHEILA RHODES **21**
3. SASHA ROBINSON **27**
4. JILL ALLISON **35**
5. MARICE WILSON **48**
6. ERICA LACY-HENDERSON **67**
7. RENEE BUCKNER **83**
8. SHEQUITA LEE-BOGLE **91**
9. ALECIA TAMEKO **99**
10. TONSHAY THERESA **109**
11. TONI HENDERSON-MAYERS **122**
12. LESLIE EPPS **138**
13. SHONDA ORLICIA **146**
14. APRIL DELILLY…**158**

Real Divas Win ™ Volume #1

1
TIFFANY A. GREEN
JUST ME

Real Divas Win. So, what's this all about? God gave me Real Divas Win to simply highlight women from everywhere. I believe in my heart that many of the women who are winning are still hidden in the bush, peeking out and just waiting to be showcased. So, allow me to introduce myself. I am Tiffany Aundriana Green. I am 42 years old, raised in Chicago and now reside in Atlanta, GA. I have 2 grown children and 4 grandchildren. I would say I have had a blessed life overall. Of course, many of us, even in our blessings still have faced challenges in life. One thing I learned in my many years on earth is that when you are destined to win, the devil will find every way possible to destroy you to the point that you don't realize you have a purpose.

In my childhood I was often teased about the way I looked, which gave me permission to think I was never good enough. I wanted to blend in with pretty girls. Well of course, because I was made to feel like I was not one of the pretty girls. I was teased every day I went to school and even on the weekends by the kids in the neighborhood who claimed to be my friends. At this age, I had no idea this was a form of bullying. I've experienced many things in my life that I know was proposed to destroy my self-esteem, my heart, and who God created me to be.

You name it I've experienced it. I was a teenage mom as well as a single mom, been in abusive relationships, married at an early age and then a widow before I turned 30 after my husband was murdered, and so on. One major blessing I received was being introduced to the power of God through Jesus Christ, at an early age. I accepted Jesus Christ as my Lord and Savior. We were raised Catholic up to around 1986 when my mom got saved and accepted Christ. Although I was forced to go to church it was the best thing I could have ever experienced. Being around, seeing and feeling the power of God showed me who he truly was. Although I didn't know a lot, one thing I knew was that Christ was very real. I would watch my mom pray and see things in our lives change. Watching my mom get up before the sun came up and walk around the house and pray in the holy spirit and pray over us every morning was something to see. We thought she was crazy, but today, I can write this chapter and say, it was all in God's plan. Gods plan was always for me to win. No matter what decisions I made, no matter how I felt, no matter how many names I had been called, no matter how many family members talked about us and wrote us off, God's plan has always reigned in my life. After my husband was murdered in 2003, I began seeking my own personal relationship with God. Now we all know just because you attend church on Sundays does not mean you have a relationship. I started seeking God for my own understanding and truth. I didn't know exactly how to pray. But I started watching Christian television and taking notes and apply the word of God to my life. I lost my mom in 2005, and truly had no one to depend on but the power of God and the Holy Spirit. Starting with just simply spending time with God made all the difference in the world. Believing and trusting 100% in Jesus, I can stand here today and say, I'm a Real Diva and I am Winning.

I BELIEVE IN MY HEART THAT MANY OF THE WOMEN WHO ARE WINNING ARE STILL HIDDEN IN THE BUSH, PEEKING OUT AND JUST WAITING TO BE SHOWCASED.

MY WINS

Before I sought out God and his goodness and love I had no idea who I truly was and who he created me to be. When you truly discover the real you, from that point on there's nothing that can stop you. I have accomplished things in my life I never imagined I could do on my own. I've always had great jobs, good income never lacked anything. When God revealed the true me, I discovered I was truly a successful entrepreneur. Now, let's take a twist in this story and get to the real deal.

I have talked about some of the things I've been through that were meant to cause me to become nothing but, now I need to tell you about my wins. Isn't this the reason for the book anyway? I have gifts that God, yes, I said God has launched on the inside of me that I did not have to go to school for. Let's get this clear, I don't have a degree. I attended college but didn't finish. In 2006 I dived into the world of photography. I've built a very impressive portfolio and have been a professional photographer for 12 years now, I have captured wedding images for brides locally, nationally and internationally including Nassau, Bahamas & Rivera Maya. Mexico. From photography, custom design and capturing thousands of wedding images, I tapped into an amazing gift offering a large variety of marketing materials for entrepreneurs and businesses.

Let's talk about the gift of writing. I've been writing since I was a child. In my late 20's I revisited my love for writing, and I started journaling daily as well as writing poetry. Then finally attempted to start writing my memoir about my life story. I never finished the book, but I acquired this passion to support writers and authors. I started a social networking site called Black Writers Space™ in 2007. This was around the time when My Space was popular. I had no idea what I wanted to do in the literary industry, but I knew that I wanted to create a platform and support writers. I grew the site to about 500 members, it was cool, I wanted to create a place for writers to gain resources and showcase their works. The site ended; however, Black Writers Space continued to evolve and grow. We are still growing on social media on Facebook, Periscope, Instagram, Twitter, and YouTube. And yes, you can google Black Writers Space, we are absolutely in the search engine.

I met a guy named Girard McClendon, and after telling him about my plans for BWS, he suggested I start a blog talk radio show. After getting over my fear of doing it, guess what? I did it. The show grew rapidly and was very successful. Yes, little me started a radio show and interviewed local authors and some popular celebrities and songwriters. I hosted my first spoken word event in 2012. Since then, I now offer consulting and publishing services for authors who want to self-publish their books. I am passionate about teaching authors the business of publishing. You can always find me across social media live streaming about publishing or business at any given time.

In my many horrible decisions in relationships, now I am truly winning in that area. After bumping my head too many times I decided to let go and let God. My prayer has always been not for God to send me a husband but for him to prepare me. I never wanted to sound like one of those desperate women who was always praying for God to send them a husband. After all this time my prayer was still God prepare me for him. This one day, I asked God to send him, and he did. Sometimes we can be in the way of what God is trying to do because we keep trying to do things our way. We connected a week after that. I am recently engaged and sooooo happy with my fiancé who is also an author. I am looking forward to spending the remainder of my years with him and enjoying life together. Seeing so many women who are taking their rightful place in business and entrepreneurship, I wanted to launch a brand that celebrated women. I created The Beautiful Boss which will be followed by some major projects very soon to launch in 2019. Finally, Real Divas Win, this book launched the start of this movement, brand and whatever else God gives me for this brand. I purposely did not charge a fee for authors to opt into this volume simply because I wanted this to be an opportunity like no other. I understand that the ground level of something holds major weight. With that being said, I wanted women who were serious and simply ready for 2018. This will be the first of many volumes in this series that will unleash the hidden gems of women who have amazing gifts, stories, and influence to introduce to the world. Each story is destined to be extremely unique with the major goal of empowering, uplifting and inspiring not just women, but the world.

    I know that 2018 is the year of winning. The truth is, Real Divas do Win. Search your story and find your wins. We get so distracted by the downfalls and totally forget about the wins. Wins are what keeps us going. Wins give us hope. Wins connect us and lead us to our destiny, period. I believe no matter what you started and did not finish, you need to make up your mind and purpose to finish and win. Only you can stop you from completing what you were destined to be in life.

Tiffany A. Green-Hood
http://flow.page/iamtiffanyagreen

2
SHIELA RHODES

The scariest time for me would have to be figuring out how to start my life over after 21yrs of marriage. I was a housewife and mother of 7, grandmother of 13 a good and faithful wife and mother. My wedding vows meant everything to me, I made them to God, and I didn't want to let God down. We did everything together. You didn't see one without the other. My husband was my best friend and my lover and in the blink of an eye he became somebody I didn't even know.

Let me introduce myself I'm Mrs. Sheila Keyes Rhodes the youngest of 6 girls the 7th of 9 children. My husband and I met because he worked with my sister. From the beginning he was determined that I would be his wife. I even moved out of Illinois for a year. As soon as he got wind that I was back in town he came and found me. We were together for 3 months before we got married January 15,1999 in downtown Chicago City Hall while he was on vacation. And we never left each other side.

That man did everything right. He opened doors, carried groceries, and catered to my every need. If I thought I wanted it I got it plus some and the love making was amazing to say the least. We acted like high school kids' multiple times a day several days a week. I upheld all my wifely duties cooked, cleaned, took care of the kids, managed the bills, you know the usual. Suddenly, everything started changing, the attention I was getting became less and less. So, I'm thinking who it is he cheating with? This happened twice in the past, I can't prove it but I know it. I packed my things and moved out I deserved better than this so I left. He kept coming to my house until he worked his way back in and was once again living with me.

> *MY WEDDING VOWS MEANT EVERYTHING TO ME I MADE THEM TO GOD AND I DIDN'T WANT TO LET GOD DOWN.*

Over a 7yr period everything really went downhill everything completely stopped. But I think the worst thing that happened was when he told me to go do whatever I needed to do for myself for sex because he didn't get anything out of it. It was like a ton of bricks hit me. What kind of man would say something like that to his wife? At first, I tried to act like it didn't hurt going along with the I love you so much I just don't want you to suffer crap. Then I found all the women he had been so chit chatty with over his Facebook inbox. I moved us from a three-bedroom home into a one-bedroom apartment to force him to sleep in our room he made a pallet on the front room floor. Every word is an argument there's no emotional connection anymore. I prayed and I prayed for some answers, so I used his illness as an excuse for him being mean and cold. But truthfully that was no reason for it. I also used that for me staying I didn't want him to die alone.

One day after talking to my Pastor Eryk F. Hood of Full Impact Ministries, I received some real clarity from one of his sermons. Then I woke up one morning and God said, he's not about to die and your children are grown. I didn't put you here to suffer you can't fix anything that's broken but you so that's what I want you to work on. I'm obedient so I started looking at my life. I apologized to my husband and children for expecting them to give me something they aren't willing to give love and loyalty. I forgave them for the disrespect but now it's time to move on. It's hard and I would be lying if I said I wasn't scared. I gave away a lot of good years. And now it's time for me to take care of me. So that means I'm leaning on the Lord and his word. Because without my faith I have nothing. I don't know where this road will lead but wherever I stop I will embrace it with open arms.

I just want any young lady out there going thru to know trust in the Lord with all your heart he will get you thru. As a result, I'm writing a street novel, a book of poetry, and this book. I am looking into other business venture to keep myself afloat. The Lord always make a way for me I'm strong and so are you. I found happiness again in my self-something I have up trying to please everyone else. It's hard for people to understand what went wrong. But guess what I loved it and still don't know why he changed like he did. I am grateful to God for my strength to move on and hold my head up while I do so. This is my life and I'm going to continue to love and rejoice in it. I've moved to Florida and starting life over, this time I'm living.

3
SASHA ROBINSON
MY MOVES GOD'S PLAN

I heard someone say if you want to make God laugh tell him your plans. I know he must've had a good laugh dealing with me, because none of my plans worked, until now. I've always enjoyed writing, and been very good at it, I sat it down for many years. When I was 10 years old it was my dream to go to Howard University and study journalism. But as my mom and most other older black women say I started "smelling' myself" and decided to get my own place and start working right after high school. I couldn't wait to be able to say I was grown.

    I spent 10 years bouncing from job to job and experimenting with a pyramid scheme after pyramid scheme before I finally decided to attend college with the intent to finish. I graduated with my Associate degree in Criminal Justice in 2014 and began working as a corrections officer 1 month after graduation. Most single mothers with two children would have been content with this life, but I still wasn't fulfilled and quite unhappy. I was fearful every day going to work. I had a female captain that hated my guts, and I didn't know from one day to the next whether I was going to be set up by another officer or fired. One morning I rolled over after working a stressful double shift, looked at the clock and noticed that I was an hour late to work. I pulled the covers over my head and went back to sleep. I couldn't take being in that environment another day. Please don't try that at home but at that moment I decided that I was going to work somewhere that made me happy, or not work at all. Little did I know with that affirmation that my faith was awakening.

    Two months after I abruptly quit the job from hell, I found the one that would ultimately land me where I am today. Right before Christmas, I started working for one of the top jewelry companies in the U.S. and I was ecstatic! Working retail during the holidays was stressful, but I thrived in the hustle and bustle of holiday shoppers. The idea and the challenge of earning commissions excited me, and I killed my goals. Within 6 months of starting with the company, I had been promoted and was well on my way to managing my own store. The only thing that would more greatly improve my chances of making this dream a reality, I would have to move. Once I made the decision to move, it happened fast. Before I knew it, I had a U-haul packed, and was headed to Louisville Kentucky, with my two daughters and my mom in tow. I was scared but I knew if I wanted more, I had to step out of my comfort zone and step out on faith. When people think of faith, they have a one-dimensional view. There are levels of faith. The level I was on when I moved was the basic level. The level that says, "I know God is with me." But it isn't until you really go through something that you hit the real level, that deep level. It seemed like once I got there and got settled, everything just shook up and fell to the ground. I hated the store I transferred to with a passion. The people that I worked with weren't excited about working. I remember filling in at a store on the outskirts of Louisville that was like the store I came from. The store was in urgent need of an assistant manager. I asked myself "Why didn't they send me to this store, so I could have my position right now?" Eventually, I quit and began doing exactly what I was doing at 19, which was hopping from job to job. My mom's health began to deteriorate and instead of watching her suffer still trying to work, I decided to take care of everything. I eventually found myself working two full-time jobs and still sinking in debt. This was the lowest point of my life. The only thing that kept me from going back to my hometown, and what was comfortable with was the relationship I was building with Christ. I had found a church in Louisville, where I was growing, and I couldn't see myself going back to what was easy, just because what I was seeing was hard. That's not what faith is about.

WHEN PEOPLE THINK OF FAITH, THEY HAVE A ONE-DIMENSIONAL
VIEW. THERE ARE LEVELS OF FAITH. THE LEVEL I WAS ON WHEN I MOVED WAS THE BASIC LEVEL. THE LEVEL THAT SAYS, "I KNOW
GOD IS WITH ME.

I got back to writing and started a prayer journal. My prayer journal alone could very well be a book because I started writing in the heart of my storm and finished it in victory. I carry it with me in my purse, so whenever I feel my faith wavering, I can open it up and see the miracles that God performed in my life at a time when I thought all hope was lost. In starting my prayer journal, I began to write short stories. Before I knew it, I had written a play and a book, with at least 5 other ideas for books written down. Through my trials and tribulations, God revealed to me my purpose. If I would have turned back to what was comfortable, I would've never discovered who God really is, how far my faith could go, and what the gift that he placed within me could do. Looking back at when I was working in the store and wondering why I couldn't have started there and been the assistant manager, I can smile. Sometimes God will put what you think you want in your face and reveal to you something greater. It is up to you to accept it or fight it. I know now, that leaning on Jesus is the best way to go. He tells us in his word that his thoughts are not our thoughts, and his ways are not our ways. I understand that now. I made my moves, but God had his plan.

Facebook: Sasha Robinson
Facebook Sincerely Sasha (@Lasasharobinson502)
Instagram: Sincerelysasha_theauthor

Real Divas Win ™ Volume #1

Periscope: Sinerelysasha.tv
YouTube: Sincerely Sasha

4
JILL ALLISON

As she rushed into the house; after praying all the praying all the way home, that her mother was not sitting at the kitchen table. She opened the door slowly, peaked her head inside and to her surprise, the house was dark. She scurried to the bathroom and quickly shut the door behind her. She peeled her pants and undergarments away as fast as she could and plopped down on the toilet. She tried her best to squeeze out some pee. it felt like her bladder was full! Finally, a trickle! Oh my! She did not expect it to burn. She Tried to stop the stream of strong-smelling urine in hopes that the burning would stop but her vagina was sore, and it felt swollen. She could barely use the tissue to wipe because it stung her precious parts. She had the presence of mind to run warm water on a towel and press it against her vagina for relief. Is THIS what everyone was so excited about?

Is THIS what IT was supposed to be like?! She was not pleased at all with the events of the evening. It was such a painful, uncomfortable feeling and she had no idea what to do.

From all the discussion she had heard in school there was no way THIS was what they all were talking about! Couldn't be! And if so, how could she continue doing that? After all, he would expect her to. He was older and could have had anyone he wanted but he wanted her. She had to please him. If she didn't, he might leave her. Her thoughts and emotions were all over the place! She had so many unanswered questions. What next? If she was to continue doing this with him would it get better? What if she didn't want to? How would he feel about her then? Would he still like her? What if her mom found out? What if she got pregnant? What if she contracted an STD? They didn't use protection.

She was afraid, and tears begin to roll down her face. Oblivious to her surroundings she began to sob quietly. Her mind wandered to her usual feelings of being alone and lost! This was a familiar and frequent series of emotions. She seemed to always feel displaced when she wasn't sure about the choices she had made. This would often sink her into a dark depression and isolation. This moment would prove no different. The noise of her mom's footsteps coming down the hall snapped her out of her tearful regret.

"Jill, is that you? Where have you been?" "I was out with my friends," she quickly answered. "I'm getting ready for bed. I'll be out in a bit," she stammered as she wiped the tears away. She hurried and turned on the shower and hopped in to try to wash away the events of the day. She had come to a crossroad that she would soon find that she was in no way prepared for. She had given away one of her most precious gifts without ever considering the repercussions of that decision. She was never good at decision making to begin with and the lack of understanding of how to count the cost of such a choice would prove to change the entire trajectory of her young life. It would lead her down a path of many more bad decisions and regrets. It would take many years for her to understand that the culmination of every choice, every mistake and every tear would all work in her favor to bring her to an expected end. Although young and clueless; sad and depressed being deeply embedded in her spirit was a resilience that would teach her to thrive despite her circumstances.

Jill would learn very early in life how God had built her to overcome some of the worst circumstances that would debilitate many but only serve as fuel to Jill's tenacious nature to survive and ultimately win! She didn't know it at the time but her rough beginnings was preparation for building her into an unstoppable force. Though she was born a seed of rejection, God would orchestrate the right and wrong people to cross her path and bring her to her place of destiny!

It was the early '70s and Irene and her good sister friend Shirley sat at the kitchen drinking their usual Saturday morning cup of coffee along with a cigarette. They were having girl talk when a tv ad caught Irene's attention. This ad had the most beautiful, 255 chubby toddler she had ever seen wearing a peach polka dot dress. There was a 1-800 number going across the screen asking for qualified couples to call in and adopt children. Irene told her sister friend to hurry up and get a pencil to take down the number because she was going to adopt this baby! Her friend Shirley burst into laughter and reminded her that the ad asked for QUALIFIED COUPLES! Irene ignored her and instructed her to get the name of the agency and the number down before the commercial went off. Shirley wrote down the number but kept informing her friend of how unqualified she was to adopt this baby. "First of all,

Irene, you don't have a husband. They said they were looking for couples. Next, you don't have any money. How are you planning to pursue an adoption? You would need a lawyer and you have NO MONEY for that! AND, where in the world would you put this child? Your house is full already!" Irene was currently a foster mom who was also on the emergency list to receive children whenever DCFS needed to place them immediately. She had just taken immediate custody of 3 children in her small 3bedroom home. They were the children of a woman she knew from the neighborhood who had a gambling and drinking problem. Irene had taken these children in the past so whenever their mom was arrested or in trouble, she would be the first call the agency would make. Despite already having 3 children, being divorced, living on a fixed income and having just a 3rd grade education, Irene had one simple question for her friend..." will you help me get her or not?" Shirley reluctantly agreed to help, and they started working on the plan immediately. Shirley had an acquaintance who put her in touch with a lawyer and that Monday morning, they called and set up an appointment to meet with him. The lawyer was a middle aged, very accomplished family court lawyer and dealt with these kinds of situations often. As he sat and listened to Irene's desire to adopt and the specificities of this case, it was clear to him that this would be an uphill battle. In the interest of not wasting any more of his own time he advised Irene to reconsider. He explained how this was nearly an impossible task and how costly it would be. He encouraged her to continue her work with foster children and to possibly revisit adopting if her situation changed. Without even a hiccup, Irene asked him did he think he could get it done at all in-spite of the challenges. He was caught completely off guard and continued sharing the difficulties of such a case but said that it wasn't impossible. That's all Irene needed to hear. She asked how much it would cost to retain him and to get started. Not expecting her to be able to come up with the fees, he wrote down some numbers on a piece of paper and handed it to her. She looked at the numbers, stood up, shook his hand and told him that he would be hearing from her soon. Totally stunned but not surprised at her friend's determination, Shirley continued to talk to Irene on the way home about how hard this entire ordeal would be on her and her family. Irene firmly explained to Shirley that her mind was made up and that she had no intentions of changing it. She told Shirley to either get on board completely or to get off. Irene had laser focus and tunnel vision when it came to something she wanted. She never allowed her limitations to hinder her once her mind was made up. Later that day Irene called a family friend who was also the neighborhood loan shark and asked him for the money to retain the lawyer. She had called him many times before for loans and was never short or late paying him back, so he never hesitated when she called. This amount was larger than normal for Irene, so he felt compelled to ask why she needed a lawyer. She explained her plan and had also worked out a payment schedule to get the money back to him over a period of time. He, like her friend, tried his best to talk her out of this decision. He explained how she'd be paying him double what he loaned her just due to interest and asked her was it worth it. Still not convinced he told her to let him sleep on it. The next day, bright and early, Irene got the call that the family friend would bring the money by the house that afternoon. Irene immediately called Shirley with the good news and told her to set up the next appointment with the lawyer to move forward. Once news spread of what Irene was up to, family and friends alike called and visited to try and talk Irene out of this aggressive battle she had taken on. Irene had a biological daughter that she had sent for her sister to raise while she worked in Little Rock Arkansas many years ago before she arrived in Chicago, so no one could understand her decision to raise a strange baby since she hadn't even raised her own flesh and blood. Despite the naysayers and the negativity, one thing was clear; nothing was going to stop Irene from making this desire a reality. In the coming weeks, Shirley and Irene worked closely with the lawyer to locate the agency and start the paperwork to getting this beautiful toddler who was once an 1800- adopt me ad. Irene could barely read and write so Shirley and the lawyer did most of the paperwork. Because of Irene's illiteracy the lawyer had to prep her for hearings and to go before judges. The lawyer had to explain most of the documents and the steps they'd have to go through to get to the point of adoption. The baby, who would become known as Jill Shirley Allison, was born with a few medical issues. So besides being a warrant of the state, she was also in terrible need of surgeries and medical attention. She was born partially blind in one eye and with digestive challenges. Due to Irene's limited funds, the lawyer convinced Irene that her best course of action would be to get Jill as a foster child for the state to finance her medical problems and for them to pursue the adoption after Jill's health was in a better state. Irene agreed to this and the courts moved to allow Irene to take Jill in under foster care. Finally, Irene had this baby in her home and was well on her way to becoming Jill's adoptive mother. Jill wouldn't know any of her back story until she became a teenager. The knowledge of what she initially viewed as a horrible start to her struggling life would almost take her out. Jill peeked outside the bathroom door to see if the coast was clear. She ran to her bedroom, closed the door and sunk deep within the covers of her bed. She quietly sobbed into her pillow until she had drifted off to sleep. She was no longer a virgin and the thought of what was next was too much to face. Sleep was always the answer for Jill because it absolved her from the responsibilities of her choices, even if for a short time. Despite how many nights she cried herself to sleep over bad decisions, God had filled her with an unstoppable anointing to live even when she felt like dying.

Regardless to odds that all seemed stacked against her, time and resilience would prove what was inevitable.

She was born to WIN!

In the meantime, connect me with at jillallison661@gmail.com
FB @ iamjallisonart
IG @ iamjallison

Real Divas Win ™ Volume #1

5
MARCIE WILSON
WINNING AS A WIFE

"But the Holy Spirit produces this kind of fruit in our lives: love, joy, peace, patience, kindness, goodness, faithfulness, gentleness, and self-control. There is no law against these things!" Galatians 5:22-23

Every fall, my family takes our annual trip to the apple orchard, it's our time to not only pick our favorite apples, but it's a time to bond. Each year we wait in anticipation to pick those gala and honey crisp apples straight from the vine. We get to ride the tractor out to the middle of the farm and once we depart, we get the opportunity to walk up and down the aisles in search of the perfect apples. These aren't your ordinary apples. They are juicy and free from pesticides and chemicals; they haven't been coated with wax to make them shine; they're pure and straight from the vine.

In taking this trip, I couldn't help but to think about how we as Winning Wives are like these trees. As a Winning Wife, our characteristics resemble the apple trees because we were created to produce good fruit. These apple trees produce good fruit for the enjoyment and benefit of others. What they bring out impacts everyone who encounters it. The same is for us, we produce so that we can give. We are electric, and everything connected to us should bloom, especially our marriages. The apples didn't just appear on the vine, they had to grow to become the perfect piece of fruit. It took planting, nurturing and growing. Winning Wives realize that it takes time for you and your spouse to become one, it doesn't happen overnight. You must put in the work to build that bond. The apples only grow on the trees so that someone could pick them, and more cannot grow until one has been picked from the vine. Apple trees realize that the more fruit they give away, the more fruit grows. And on the contrary, more fruit cannot grow if the vine is occupied. Winning Wives we cannot grow until we give the good fruit we are generating away. It would be foolish for an apple tree to say, "I don't want to give my apples away because someone may not use it correctly," That's how we sound when we don't give our fruit of love, joy, peace, kindness, goodness, faithfulness, gentleness and self-control to our spouses. Even when they don't deserve it, give it to them anyway! Truth is, when we think he doesn't deserve it, that's when he needs it the most. God never withholds his love from us. He gives it freely and so should we. Winning Wives produce and give with the understanding that the more I give; the more God gives me.

"The generous will prosper; those who refreshes others, will themselves be refreshed." Proverbs 11:25

Ironically, Paul, the author of the book of Galatians calls it the fruit of the Spirit but list 9 traits. From one virtue flows eight more attributes.

The first item named is the fruit- Love. From love flows joy, peace, patience, kindness goodness, faithfulness, gentleness and self-control. The word for love as described in this verse is "agape" which is God's kind of love. It's the highest form of love. It's the kind of love that God the Father has for you, to love you so much that He sacrificed His only Son for you. It's the kind of Love Jesus has for you that He was willing to die that you might live. It's the kind of Love that the Holy Spirit has, that of all the dwelling places, in or out of this world, He chooses to live inside you. The kind of love that is patient, kind, does not envy, or boast or is proud, easily angered or keeps a record of wrong. The kind of love that always protects, always trusts, always hopes, always persevere (1 Corinthians 13). And from this, joy flows; peace flows; patience flows. And every Winning Wife exudes love because she knows that she has been saturated in God's love.

This is a lesson I had to learn If I wanted to win in my marriage. Once I accepted just how much God really loved me, it made it easier to love myself. Loving yourself helps to set healthy boundaries. My time and energy are precious, and it gave me the freedom to choose how I would use it and who I would allow in space. I learned to love me enough to let the toxic people go. When I realized who I was and how much I was worth, the game changed. I was able to make "me" a priority. I had spent so much time making sure everyone else was together, that I had neglected making sure I was together. This could no longer be the norm. So, I accepted God's love and it gave me the strength and courage to love myself without feeling guilty.

"Taking care of yourself isn't vanity, it's for your sanity."

This new-found love for myself, gave me the tools I needed to love my husband. I admit, when I first walked into my marriage we weren't winning in marriage; In fact, we were losing. As a result, we experienced some hardships and setbacks in love. My husband and I went through a Journey of Love, that placed us at the crossroads; we could either divorce or work it out. And at that time the path was bent towards divorce. We had to have some hard conversations and make some tough decisions because both roads would require much work. After much arguing, crying and praying, we traveled the difficult road of restoration. During that time, I was able to use the love strategies I learned from God to transform and win in my marriage. (To read our story and to learn how to use prayer, affirmations and scriptures to change the trajectory of your marriage;

get a copy Journey to Love at MarcieWilson.com, Amazon, Barnes & Noble and all online distributors. Available in paperback and eBook,)

"Love is Choice!"

THIS IS A LESSON I HAD TO LEARN IF I WANTED TO WIN IN
MY MARRIAGE. ONCE I ACCEPTED JUST HOW MUCH GOD REALLY LOVED ME, IT MADE IT EASIER TO LOVE MYSELF.
LOVING YOURSELF HELPS TO SET HEALTHY BOUNDARIES.
MY TIME AND ENERGY ARE PRECIOUS, AND IT GAVE ME THE FREEDOM TO CHOOSE HOW I WOULD USE IT AND
WHO I WOULD ALLOW IN THAT SPACE?

Winning in love created a solid foundation to give devotion to my husband. Not to say that I am doing everything perfect, but it has given me the foundation

I need to make better decisions in all aspects of my life. When I decided to let love reign, it made it easier for the other parts of the fruit to fall into place.

Choosing love made it easier to establish good soil for the rest of the fruit to flourish. Winning in love became the segway to winning in joy. Joy isn't happiness because happiness is based upon what is happening around you. Your mood is determined by your surroundings. If my environment is sad, it has the power to make me sad. But joy is a state of eternal bliss. Joy is learning to be content in all situations. When you win in joy, your circumstances will no longer dictate your emotions, instead you control how you react. When I began to really understand the institution of marriage, I realized that it was greater than us being in love, but it was attached to our purpose. When we discovered the purpose of our marriage, it brought my heart joy! It doesn't mean that every day we are happy, but every day I live blessed. Blessed to love and blessed by being loved.

"For this reason, a man will leave his father and mother and be united to his wife, and the two will become one flesh" Genesis 19:5

A few years ago, my marriage took a blow. The kind that shatters and break things such as trust, commitment and bonds. I was certain our marriage was over. That's when our Journey to Love began. I was challenged by God to pray & encourage my husband to 30 Days. From that journey God produced fruit in our relationship. I was able to build up a reservoir of love and to see my husband as God sees him. It was eye opening, but I wasn't quite ready to give my fruit away. To produce is one thing but giving it away was a whole new thing. Why? Because I still wasn't convinced that my husband deserved it. In fact, I was holding my good fruit as ransom and punishment. When you produce something that's good, you realize how much work it takes, and your instinct is to want to keep it to yourself, especially when you feel they don't deserve it. God created an opportunity for me to give it away. After seeing my husband through God's eyes, it moved me to compassion. Compassion turned into forgiveness and forgiveness led to a deeper love. God had configured our situation in such a way, that I had to begin to show him patience, kindness and self-control. "Love never gives up!"- 1 Corinthians 13:7 When I was angry with my husband and the state of our marriage was in jeopardy, God allowed tragedy to strike. After a lengthy battle of sickness, his mother passed away. My husband had spent most of that year traveling back and forth to be with her. His hurt became my hurt. I had to be patient with him. I had to learn to love him past his pain. I became a student of Fred and learned what he needed and then I prayed and asked God to show me how to be that wife. And He did! I was able to share my fruit of kindness, gentleness and goodness with my husband. And I found joy in doing it. God used this situation to draw us closer together and He gave me an opportunity to bear good fruit. During the same time, I was taking care of my mother who was diagnosed with pancreatic cancer. My siblings and I became overnight caregivers. Now my pain had become his pain. We were both wounded and didn't have the proper time to grieve his mother before my mother died. In less than six months we had lost 2 parents. The suffering was real. But God allowed the toughest times in our lives to help us flourish in our marriage. God used tragedy to make us one. A few months after my mother passed my father-in-law became ill and the cycle began all over again. In 3 year, we had lost all 3 remaining parents. This pushed me into a new life, that I wasn't quite ready for. I had no living parents, and my children did not have any living grandparents. I didn't know if I could survive because I still needed my parents, I still had questions. But the comfort of God helped me to stand strong in the face of uncertainty. The gentleness we displayed to one another gave us the assurance that we would survive. The grief is undeniable, and the pain is solid, but despite it all, I choose joy! I Choose Joy!

When love is established, and joy is evident, you can live in peace. The moment I chose joy, A Fresh Wind was established. I was challenged to think positive for 30 days and during that time, I developed a new mind-set and a way of living. A Fresh Wind is a way of establishing a positive mental attitude about all circumstances. It's not ignoring your reality, but it's choosing to see it from another perspective so that you can win. Sometimes, you just need to take a moment to inhale and exhale and take in A Fresh Wind. It brings you back to your center and creates balance. It allows you to live in peace, even though chaos is present. It allows you to be patient with yourself and your husband. It gives you the freedom to sprinkle kindness like confetti and to share goodness with all you meet. It requires Real Divas to be faithful to what God has created you to do. Realizing that it will be a tumultuous journey, but it will be well worth the trek. Emotions will try to dictate your actions, but self-control is necessary. When we master our emotions and learn to be proactive instead of reactive, we win. Winning Wives understand that it's our connection to God and other real divas that help us to produce good fruit. Being connected to the vine and having healthy relationships aid us to bear much fruit. I noticed on the apple tree that the best fruit were high up on the vine. The farmer told us that those apples were juiciest and best because they had strong roots, and they were able to grow tall. They grew in the direction of the sun. It was the sun that the apples gravitated towards. The higher they grew, the more connected they needed to be to the vine, that's their strength. Winning Wives recognize that their strength also comes from being connected to the vine- "I am the true vine and My Father is the gardener. He cuts off every branch that does not bear fruit and prunes every branch that does bear fruit so that it can bear fruit." (John 15:5). Our marriages grow when we allow God to be at the center. Becoming one flesh means that you allow Him to remove anything that doesn't bear good fruit and to prune every branch so that it can bear more fruit. Pruning hurts because it means He will cut off some stuff and if we're honest, some things we like to hold on to because it has become a part of us. Old habits are hard to break. If we look at the wife in Proverbs 31, we see that she was the epitome of a woman and she was winning as a wife. I studied her and found out that Winning requires work, dedication, vision, fortitude and connections. Who you are connected to matters and your network should make you better?

Empowered Women Empower other women.

The Essence of a Winning Wife "is clothed with strength and dignity, and she laughs without fear of the future. When she speaks, her words are wise, and she gives instructions with kindness.
Proverbs 31: 25-26

I have been able to win in many areas, some victories are small, and others are huge, but it requires me to take a self-inventory and to be honest with myself. It requires that I make necessary changes to become better and it opens the door for me to help others win. Winning isn't just for you, but it's about you helping others to win too!

Real Divas produce other winning Divas.

On Facebook, I wanted to see more women encouraging other women, so I created a group to help us keep in touch. I thought it would be a place for my small circle and before I knew it had grown to over 2,500 women overnight. It took on a life of its own and now we have dynamic women, all races and ethnicities, from all over the world, encouraging each other daily. This proves that God will use you to do great things. (Join the movement on Facebook. Join Today's Leading Lady and let's empower one another.)

It's time for self-reflection. Grab a journal or download a journal app on your phone and ask yourself the following questions. Write down your honest answers and pray about what changes you need to make. Solicit a prayer partner to hold you accountable and help you celebrate your victories.

Here are a few winning questions to ask yourself:
Diva,
- ✓ How's your relationships? Have you prayed for your husband? Marriage?
- ✓ What would you like to see in your relationship?

- ✓ What fruit do you need to work so that you can win? (Love, Joy, Peace, Patience, Goodness, Gentleness, Kindness, Faithfulness, Self-control) Be honest with yourself and be willing to make the necessary changes.
- ✓ What are you producing?
- ✓ How are your connections?
- ✓ Who are you empowering?
- ✓ Are you celebrating your wins?

If you are single and desire to be married, these are some tools you can also use. Begin to pray for your future husband and that God will bring you two together.

Don't forget to celebrate your WINS!

This Chapter was Written by Marcie Wilson CEO (Chief Encouragement Officer) of A Fresh Wind

Let's Connect:

For Booking
Marcie@MarcieWilson.com
Blog & Website
MarcieWilson.com
Facebook
Personal: Marcie Stowers- Wilson
Fan Page: A Fresh Wind (Like this page for daily inspiration)
Group: Today's Leading Lady (Join our group of Empowered Women, Empowering other women)
Instagram
Personal: MarcieWilson17
Inspiration: a_fresh_wind
Twitter @afreshwind

6
ERICA LACY-HENDERSON
I AM GOOD ENOUGH

It's May of 1987, Prom has come and gone, and it's my Senior graduation day. One of the most exciting days of my life and I just made 18 years old!! I graduated from Thornton Township High School in Harvey, IL which is in the South Suburbs of Chicago, IL. where I spent the first (formative years) 12 years of my life. What a beautiful summer it's going to be because I am "grown", going to college and about to go to be an independent woman and raise my baby! Oh wait, did I mention I was pregnant for the second time and my baby boy is due in September 1987. Let me go back 7 months- October 1986 when I told my mother that I was pregnant by my high school sweetheart who was away at Florida A&M University and we are getting married when I graduate high school. The look on my mother's face told me that an open hand smack in the face was on its way. But that did not happen instead there was dead silence for what seemed like 24 hours but was only a 30second pause for her to reach inside of herself and gather herself because she was now an ordained minister under Metaphysical teaching. That saved my face to her hand action. That was one of the hardest things that I have ever had to tell my mother, after all the lessons, all the conversations about birth control, all my "religious" teachings, all the conversations about waiting until marriage to have sex-don't become a statistic: I was pregnant at 17 years of age. So now imagine the look on my Father's face, who was re-married and raising another family with 2 girls, my little sisters. Abortion was not an option in my eyes, however, at 17 years of age, I was still a minor and my opinion and thoughts did not matter even though it was "my body". But I had been "there" before. You know that feeling that your "no" is taken as a "yes" and you feel like your hands are tied and you have no voice and if you do no one cares what you have to say?! That moment where you think "finally, someone to love me like I want to be loved with no judgments of my childhood troubles that I tried to bury deep". BUT not so, the following week my parents partnered up which was indeed rare occasion because they always argued, to take me to the Hospital to have an abortion. The day after that procedure, I was broken hearted and felt so alone, once again. My brother, who was only 1 year and 2 weeks older than I, had left in August of that summer of (1986) after he graduated from Thornridge High School off to the Navy. He was my protector, my best friend and my "dad." In lieu of my dad's in and out, on and off for the most part of our younger years. Oh, how often we wish our parents had a manual on the do's and don'ts of parenting, BUT they don't. So, the feelings of abandonment became very familiar to me. "Maybe I wasn't good enough" I would think.

At any rate, my brother filled that void, as much as he could be being a kid himself. But as a young girl growing up in the city of Chicago and then relocating to the South Suburbs for what my mother considered or had high hopes of it being "A better life" to Harvey, IL you need a male role model or a strong male presence to ward off predators. My brother Micah was that "superhero" for me. However, I digress. Little did I know that that would be the precursor to yet another pregnancy two months later. "Delight yourself also in the Lord, and HE will give you the desires of your heart" (Psalms 37:4) In my heart, I really wanted my baby that my parents encouraged me to abort. But I did not know that having my baby that my boyfriend (KB) and I talked about would be the demise of our three-year relationship. Yep, I had broken up with the guy that I thought would never cheat on me, hurt me or leave me and he did just that!! When I told him, I was pregnant again he was on the first bus smoking. Now, I got to break this news to my mother again, mind you, who had just begun to live her life again as my brother and I were older and about to be an empty nester. So, she thought. That was the first time that my spiritual, independent, strong-black Queen, single mother from East St. Louis ever called me out of my birth name. My mother did not speak to me from December 1986 until approximately March 1987 (other than for household business purposes). I was lonely and felt alone as I had felt majority of my life, at 18. However, I was determined to complete high school despite the temptations to drop out and go to Business College to pursue Executive Secretary and Word Processing.

Now, here I was on May 1987 at my Senior graduation, 5 months pregnant, NO Sr. prom, No boyfriend and back to the overflowing of feelings of abandonment. "I guess I wasn't good enough again?!" was the rhetorical question I had to ask myself again. But my teachings of God allowed me to push forward and gave me the tenacity to keep going and not look back. "One day God will give me revelation as to why KB left me and his child". September 6th, 1987 at 10: 00 a.m. on a Sunday morning my SUNSHINE was born!! Dominique Lacy. Strawberry blonde-golden curls caressed his small head as his Ocean blue eyes opened to see who this vessel was that his Heavenly Father had chosen to carry him for 9 months, sing to his spirit while in the womb and read all genres of books to whom to prepare for his arrival lest his journey. The Synergy that we had was God-given! "Wow, hopefully I will be good enough for this bundle of joy that God has entrusted me with" I thought to myself as my mother stood near me with tears of joy. She was amazed at his beauty and in awe because this was the baby boy that God showed her in a dream. Three months later I took my son to the Doctor only to find out that he was blind. "Here we go again!! What am I going to do with a Blind kid at 18 years old, Lord? This job is going to be too difficult for me by myself and you let his father walk away from me. My mother is only 38 years old and living her own life. My brother is away in the Military and, I felt like my own father did not have time for me and my child because he has "his own family" with 2 younger children to take care of. Plus, why would he be available for me now when he wasn't there during those horrific years at the "Babysitters house". He's not going to help me with a blind kid! God...I AM SO ANGRY RIGHT NOW!! " This was my foolish prayer to God when I got home.... God I am so angry right now !!" This is the statement I made in my prayer to God when I got home from that Dr's appointment. Those ugly feelings of loneliness fear and abandonment creeped in again. "Am I not good enough to raise a normal child "was the question I asked. My mother told me the next day "who's report will you believe Erica? The report of the Doctors or the Report of the Lord?" So of course, you know I chose God's report because I remembered the story of Blind Bartimaeus (Mark 10:46-52) when Jesus told him to go about his way because his FAITH has made him well (to see). My faith and the faith of my praying mother, Eunice, interceding on my son's behalf, 1 year old he began seeing.

Somethings come into our lives to test that which God has already stored deep within us and at times such as that, when we have NO ONE but God to trust in and lean on we must walk in that faith and not in what we see with our physical eyes! This has been my walk from that day in the summer of 1988 until today. I was engaged to a man, twice, that I had my second child with, Ariel Anise Murphy, in 1993. This is the man that I thought God sent into my life in June 1988 to love my son Dominique as his own flesh and blood. This man taught me a lot about street life and at the same time teaching me how a lady should be valued as a Queen but that was all superficial and surface. He was cheating and every time he got caught, we had a physical altercation. At skating rinks, after church services, at the neighborhood bar, at the bowling alley, and even before formal events during New Year's Eve Galas. I became very Angry again during the pregnancy of my daughter so much so that she came into this world fearful. Police was called and involved on several occasions, but I refused to become a lifelong victim of Domestic Violence. One morning in June 1995, after a night of physically fighting, the last sign that God was keeping me and "him" when a weapon of my choosing was involved which could have landed us in prison and in the grave. This was happening in front of our 7-year-old son. I was so hurt that my son in front of my 6-year-old son, I was so hurt that my son saw me do this to the only man that he knew as his dad, that I promised on that day that my children would never see me fight and argue with another man as long as I live. The next morning when I got up for work and no sleep, I went to my mother's apartment in Chicago to tell her everything I had been going through and to ask her for forgiveness and if the children and myself could come back home. I left everything that I owned;

clothes and kid's clothes, car, and furniture and stepped out on that old faith walk again. This time I had to believe that God would grant me mercy and favor to obtain a better job/career to manage without the kid's father, who had been the major income provider. He took care of everything while I went to Business College, Community College and University. Those old feelings emerged again of "not being good enough" that he would stay committed to our family. Nope, he didn't, and I could not stay there in that negative space and feel sorry for myself. Following my mother's teachings "it's okay to cry for a night, but in the morning, you have to go and wash your face and get keep things afloat for your children!" It was hard because I thought I needed this man, but God showed me that HE was the man that I needed and that he would never leave me, nor will he forsake me! (Hebrews 13:5) We ended our Love/Hate relationship after 7 years; Involving physical and domestic violence, in June of 1995. A year later he was marrying someone else and remains married to her, beautiful lady, today with two beautiful daughters and is still a constant and consistent FATHER/DAD to my son Dominique and our daughter Ariel. In that same year, August 1995 God had moved me into one of my dream jobs/careers in Law Enforcement, as Correctional Officer making good money; enough to pay my bills without depending on a man. This is one of the attributes that my mother instilled in us. I have gone through molestations, attempted rape, domestic violence, ridicule from my own family for having four children, abortion, miscarriage, cervical cancer, two pulmonary embolisms after having major surgery, Thyroid Cancer, "daddy issues" that resulted in multiple failed engagements yet relationship woes, abandonment issues, being hurt in the church by people I called family, backstabbed by close friends and feelings unappreciated by my own children only for God to answer my life long question....

"YOU ARE GOOD ENOUGH. I ALLOWED ALL OF THESE THINGS TO HAPPEN TO YOU TO MAKE YOU STRONGER, SPIRITUALLY, PHYSICALLY, MENTALLY/EMOTIONALLY FOR WHAT I AM APPOINTING AND ANOINTING YOU TO DO FOR MY KINGDOM!! SPEAK TO MY CHILDREN SHARE YOUR STORIES WITH MY DAUGHTERS, BE AN EXAMPLE FOR THEM THAT THEY MAY SEE MY GLORY IN YOU! YOU WILL LIVE THE REST OF YOUR LIFE AS A WALKING TESTIMONY FOR ME AND WHAT I CAN DO AND WILL DO FOR THEM!! AS I HAVE GIVEN TO YOU FOUR LIVING STREAMS OF RUNNING WATER TO QUENCH YOUR THIRST FOR LOVE, AS THEY WILL LOVE YOU AS I LOVE YOU.
I AM THAT I AM!!"

So today I know my worth, I have been blessed with a man of God whom I have the privilege of calling him "Husband", Alvin Henderson. He loves my children as his own, through all my shortcomings, my faults, my trials and kisses the scars of my past because they have shaped me into the Queen that I am today! I have lived " lived in homes that I used to dream about. In what is considered to be affluent Suburban areas of Chicago, IL._ We've made well into 6 figure incomes, drove some of the finest cars. All the while endured and persevered when some of the people closest to me said that I would never amount to anything and I'd be on Public Aid all my life. Now can you imagine the hurt and pain that that caused me as a young adult? That encouraged me to press forward and more persistent to succeed. I have pursued my dreams of acting in 2011 until now. From stage-play acting/singing in community theater in Chicago to the touring cast of "The Color Purple "off-Broadway musical with Celebrities such as Angie Stone,

Vanessa Bell-Armstrong, Ann Nesby and a host of local celebrities from the Chicago. Starting our own Commercial Finance & Trucking Co., LLC. and pursuing my own Salon Studio Suites in the North Texas area - Beauty Within Salon Suites, LLC. This is the name that God gave me in a dream to encourage women to know that Beauty is within you first because that's where God is!! We as women go through many things, struggles, secret battles on the inside and dress up the outside. But once we UNDERSTAND who we are as QUEENS we can walk with our heads high and know that WE ARE MORE than enough because we are ROYALTY!!! Divas: Urban dictionary reads. "adj., to describe a person who exudes GREAT style and personality with confidence and expresses their own style and not letting other influence who they are or want to be. A person whose character makes them stand out from the rest...." Continue to WIN!!

Real Divas Win ™ Volume #1

7
Renee' Buckner Fight to Win

When we think of someone winning, we often think of someone that has achieved great exploits n life. Many measures winning by the number of material possessions one has, degrees, or popularity. But for some of us, we might not have achieved those things, but we are considered winners simply because we have survived! In a world that can be cruel and unfair, it takes a winner mentality to keep going and to survive. My story is a story of someone that was lost but eventually found her way.

As a child, I had many dreams and aspirations. My mind and body were still at the stage of innocence, and I believed that I could do whatever I wanted in this world. At the age of 15, I had my life planned out. I knew what college I wanted to go to, the career I was going to pursue. I was being raised in the church, working in ministry, and loving every bit of it. Then one day I became a victim of a sexual assault, and my life took a complete turn for the worst. The one thing in life that every woman valued because she knew she could never get back was gone. Not only gone but taken without permission. Like many women that have experienced this type of abuse, I became distanced. I didn't know who to talk or who to trust. So, I carried this burden on my own for many years. I felt ruined and no longer felt worthy. I slowly began to let go of my dreams and started excepting less than I deserved. In my mind, I felt defeated, but there was something deep in my soul that was fighting for me. It wouldn't let me completely give up, and it gave me hope that better days would come. By the age of 17 I was living on my own and paying bills. I now had the responsibility of an adult but wasn't mature enough to make adult decisions. I ended up in an abusive relationship. This did nothing but contribute to the pain and mistrust of people that I already consumed on the inside. I can remember many days of covering up my bruises, attempting to hide my situation from family and friends. I remained in that relationship for over 4 years, until I couldn't take it any longer. My self-esteem was at an all-time low. I no longer loved myself and found it difficult to love others. I became pregnant at the age of 21. My body wasn't in the condition to carry a child full term, which caused me to have a premature delivery. My child was 2lb and 2oz, I was told that she was at risk of surviving. But for some reason, I had no doubt that she would grow and become a healthy child. Once she turned two years old, I decided I needed a change of environment. That summer, I relocated to Kentucky, with my daughter, 400 dollars and everything I owned in a small U-Haul truck. I'd only visited this town a few times in my entire life, but I felt something pulling me in that direction. I knew I didn't have anyone there to help me, but I felt no fear as I embarked on this journey. I was just excited to experience a new beginning. My first year in Kentucky was difficult, nothing went according to plan. I lost jobs, faced evictions, got involved with the wrong people, and even got in trouble with the law. I attempted to go back to college to finish my degree, but even that fell through. By the age of 30, I gave birth to my second child. That relationship didn't go as I would like, and once again I was alone, raising two children. Years later I found myself sitting in my bedroom, and a feeling of exhaustion came over my body. I felt like I had no more strength to continue with life. I was tired of trying, life seemed to be nothing but a constant fight and struggle. I was ready to give up, it was then when I cried out to God. I had become somewhat angry with Him. I felt like He had left me to tackle this world on my own. I began to question God. I wanted to know why he allowed me to deal with so much heartache. Why didn't I get the picture-perfect life that He seemed to give others?"

At that moment of confusion, I picked up my bible and opened it to the book of Joshua. The first chapter and the ninth verse had already been highlighted and read, "Have I not commanded you? Be strong and courageous. Do not be frightened, and do not be dismayed, for the Lord your God is with you wherever you go." (Joshua 1:9 ESV)

. I WAS READY TO GIVE UP, IT WAS THEN WHEN I CRIED OUT TO GOD. I HAD BECOME SOMEWHAT ANGRY WITH HIM. I FELT LIKE HE HAD LEFT ME TO TACKLE THIS WORLD ON MY OWN. I BEGAN TO QUESTION GOD. I WANTED TO KNOW WHY HE ALLOWED ME TO DEAL WITH SO MUCH HEARTACHE. WHY DIDN'T I GET THE PICTURE? PERFECT LIFE THAT HE SEEMED TO GIVE OTHERS?"

After reading that verse, I realized that God had never left me, it was I that left Him. I thought I could live my life without seeking Him. I was raised in the church, but once I was on my own, I barely even prayed. I sat there thinking about all the times that I could've lost my mind, but I didn't. Even though I was a single mother, I never had to depend on anyone to make ends meet. I've always had my own and never had to settle in a relationship just to be supported. I came to realize the reason I never gave up was that God was there fighting on my behalf. I decided at that moment, that I wanted to dedicate my life back to Him. I recognized that although my road was rough, God was the reason I had made it this far. I begin to attend church more and study my bible daily. I later found a church home and got baptized and started living a life of Christ. I began to see myself the way God saw me, victorious, strong and uniquely made. Having a relationship with Jesus taught me how to not only love myself but others. I was able to release my hurt and forgive those that hurt me. I felt a new life emerging on the inside. I was gaining more confidence, I felt as if I could win after all. Once I started seeking God for direction and stopped trying to do things by my own account, my life begins to turn around. The Lord blessed me with a career that I was under-qualified for. I have been working for one of the largest insurance companies in the country for over five years. I am the founder and owner of an online business that is constantly growing. My children are gifted, blessed and healthy. Two years ago, I was appointed as a leader at my church, this experience has helped me to mature and grow even closer to Christ. I now recognize that my life was never in vain. God allowed me to go through those obstacles for a reason. There was a purpose behind the pain. I understand there is a call on my life to help other women that are facing similar situations. I am now a licensed Minister of the Gospel. Equipped to preach the Gospel of Jesus Christ. For once in life, I feel like

I'm where I belong, I am walking in my purpose. Yes, I had to fight to win, but I realized that the battle wasn't mined from the beginning. I can't take credit for my wins; I must give all the Glory to God. Without him, I would still be trying to figure life out on my own. I hope that someone reads my story and decides to surrender their fight over to Christ. He is the way, the truth, and the life. And because of Him, I am a winner.

Renee Buckner- Facebook
ah_rarefinding725

Instagram
reneebuckner5@gmail.com

8
SHEQUITA LEE
ALL PLANS CHANGE

A dream will make you pack your bags and leave a home you've known for 35 years. I woke up one day and decided I was tired of Connecticut. I was ready to experience life elsewhere, this divorced mom of two young sons, knew it was time to get the ball rolling. Once I decided on what state I wanted to move to, the planning began. Being born and raised in the city, I was used to a fast pace, but moving south, I quickly realized that things didn't move as fast as I like. It took me a little more time than I originally planned to find employment. Once I moved to Virginia the company that I finally secured employment with, informed me that the company would be moving its headquarters & my department to Detroit. The HR Recruiter asked me if I would like to join the company in Detroit, in which I gave her a quick no. There was no way I would move from Connecticut to Virginia, and then turn around and move to Detroit. That's when reality kicked in I really started to think.... Did I make the right move?

Moving to a new state, knowing absolutely anyone. I decided to dig in deep and make the situation work in my favor. I connected with several job placement agencies and online job boards. After hearing numerous times, you are overqualified, I was finally able to secure employment. After going thru that process, I realized that I really wanted to investigate my option of self-employment. Knowing that I wanted to start a business. I wrote down all the things that I am good at. Google was my best friend. I started looking up information on things on my list. Checking out what the requirements would be to open each business. From there I decided to see if there were any local networking groups for Women Entrepreneurs. I found a group of women, who were still working their 9 to 5 and running their business on the side. I read books like Who Ate My Cheese, Think and Grow Rich and several others.

After joining a local club and reading various books, I decided to see if Facebook had any book clubs and/or women's groups. To my surprise, I found numerous women in business groups to join, which is right up my alley. Once I decided which groups I wanted to join, I just sat back and evaluated what was going on in each group, I rarely engaged and almost never posted. It wasn't until 2015 that I decided to get involved in a group, and not be a fly on the wall anymore. There was a publisher in the group that had just released a collaboration a month earlier, since I am an avid reader, I decided to purchase the book in support of the ladies in the group. After purchasing the book and posting a review. An opportunity came and knocked at my door.

Would you like to become a #1 Best Selling Author? After praying on it, I decided to open the door to Opportunity. That's when reality kicked in I really started to think.... Did I make the right move?

> MOVING TO A NEW STATE, KNOWING ABSOLUTELY ANYONE. I DECIDED TO DIG IN DEEP AND MAKE THE SITUATION WORK IN MY FAVOR.

Now I was beyond excited, nervous and scared, but I knew I wanted it. But when the time came for me to start writing I started wondering how much writing I will need to do, what will I write about. As I started writing the book, I remembered my first time writing any type of novel or plot, was in the early 80's. I loved watching Dynasty a mini-series that came on TV. My Best Friend & I decided to start writing various endings to the Dynasty television show. It wasn't until the mid-to-late 90's that I started journaling, and in early 2000 I decided to start Blogging. So, writing has always been something I did, but being an author wasn't a vision of mine.

The promise of being a Published, #1 Best Selling Author was great, but that was the only promise. The visionary of the book was not going to market and promote our book for us. The additional parts of the promotion were to get a graphic with our headshot and the written notice that we are published, authors.

As time passes and I think about turning in my chapter, I start thinking let me prepare for my journey of being an author. I had a feeling that things were just starting to take off.

With the excitement of being an author, of course, you start telling everyone you know, because you are no longer an aspiring author, you are about to be a published author. Then I started thinking about all the TV interviews heck maybe we will be on Oprah. I really started to see the big picture when I thought about being a part of this book. Motivation helped me to join Toastmasters International because if I was going to meet Oprah, I wanted to know how to present & speak well. I started preparing myself by joining Toastmasters, so I started doing Podcast and Radio Interviews. Once our book was released, I started doing Vendor & Authors Exhibits and really marketing my works in this book. My mindset at the time was I am putting myself out there as much as I possibly can. No one will know who you are if you don't tell them. So never be afraid to take the steps that are needed to get you closer to your dreams!

> No one will know who you are if you don't tell them.

When I think about the downfalls, wins, struggles & victories. I look back at where I started and where I am at currently. The downfall is moving to a new state and that job that I had lined up is no longer available. But the Win was finding my footing and getting a job doing what I enjoy. I struggled to figure out how to share my first story with strangers, the victory was it was well received, and it gave me the courage to press on.

Connect with me to hear more about my journey:
Website: www.authorshequitalee.com
Email: info@authorshequitalee.com
Connect with me on Social Media
Twitter: shequitalee
Periscope: shequitalee
Facebook: ShequitaLeeMedia

9
ALECIA TAMEKO
FIND YOUR TREASURE

The 80's Birthed Me. I don't remember much of my childhood. I do remember being close with cousins, but we don't talk as much anymore. I remember dance contests, Double Dutch in the streets, family barbecues, a road trip to a Memphis family reunion and breakfast at a restaurant called Shoney's. Visiting my dad's hometown in Mississippi to meet his mother and father for the first time and my grandmother giving me the most beautiful quilt. The base was navy blue and the patches were all kinds of patterns and designs. That's the only memory I can remember of my father's parents. Besides their deaths and not having the opportunity to know more about my father side of the family. I remember sleepovers, cabbage patch dolls, Teddy Ruxpin, watching Howard The Duck, a floor model doll house, hide and seek, laughing uncontrollably just being a kid you know. I am an 80's baby, indeed. I was a child who didn't ask for much. I lived in a two-parent household for six years and then my brother was born. I really thought that was my baby, you couldn't have told me different. A father who worked hard and knew how to take care of home. A countryman from Minter, Mississippi who eats snake, deer, rabbit, chitterlings, cornbread with buttermilk like it's cereal or something, slab bacon and a host of other things that makes me do the side-eye roll and stank face. My dad provided for his family, I saw no wrong, no pain, no fear. Our family never wanted for anything. You know my father is the first man I've ever loved, and he loves my mother dearly. Did I mention my parents have been married forty years? My mother who everyone says I look like, but I think I look more like my father. My mother is beautiful in all her ways, sensitive, sassy, controlling, protective, and loving the best way a mother knows how. My mom was born in Memphis, Tennessee who came from a big family who endured her fair share of abuse growing up as well. Sixteen children my grandmother birth, but by the time I was born, there were only nine girls and three boys that I knew as my aunties & uncles. My mother knew she could shop and still does to this day. We shopped every weekend at department stores. Our closets were filled with clothing and tags hanging. We grew faster than we could wear them. I don't remember my mom working as much. You know a few jobs here and there, helping her mother doing realty. I remember home cooked meals every day. We were well-groomed children and very color coordinated, I just chuckled. My mother matches everything, from clothing to decorating. The rules growing up were going to school, don't bring home "C's", come in do your homework and keep your room clean. The memories fade, and life changed from good, bad, worse, and getting better.

Innocence was Mine and You Stole It

I was 9 years old when my virginity and innocence was stolen from me. My therapist says it could have been as early as 5 years old, but I don't remember. I was 17 and a Freshman in college dating and started to remember that I was sexually abused as a child. Imagine being a seventeen-year-old girl experiencing a rush of emotions from a kiss given by your first college boyfriend. It was good, but I didn't see stars or get aroused as you may have seen in movies. I thought it was a dream, but it felt like it had just happened yesterday that I remembered being sexually victimized by a boy I thought I could trust.

Then that boy becomes boys against my own will. I was about 12 when the abuse stopped from what I can remember. Kiss a boy and you'll like it, more like kiss a boy and it will trigger ALL your suppressed memories. The relationship with my first college boyfriend didn't last long. I was 21 years old when I lost my virginity for the second time around to the man, I thought I would spend the rest of my life with it blinded me mentally, emotionally, and physically.

Insult to Pain

The "love" of my life left me and broke up with me in a one-sentence letter. "Tweety, I had to go to Iowa but will call you when I get there." I didn't hear from him for a month. It was a rainy night when we talked on my birthday and that's when he told me he was living with the mother of his future child and had to see if it would work out. "I'm in love with you both, but I have to do this!" My grades suffered and I barely graduated from college, but I did that. First, to graduate college in my family. My parents didn't finish middle or high school. Well, I never saw my "love" again, not until he contacted me to get some things that I had packed in the basement and forgot all about. Can you believe he showed up and showed out with his son's mother and then wife? That scene was like a reality show. Car chase, police were called, oh and I was every ungodly name you can imagine. I was hurt, humiliated, embarrassed, shamed, and once again victimized.

I WAS 9 YEARS OLD WHEN MY VIRGINITY AND INNOCENCE WAS STOLEN FROM ME. MY THERAPIST SAYS IT COULD HAVE BEEN AS EARLY AS 5 YEARS OLD, BUT I DON'T REMEMBER. I WAS 17 AND A FRESHMAN IN COLLEGE DATING AND STARTED TO REMEMBER THAT I WAS SEXUALLY ABUSED AS A CHILD. IMAGINE BEING A SEVENTEEN-YEAR-OLD GIRL EXPERIENCING A RUSH OF EMOTIONS FROM A KISS GIVEN BY YOUR FIRST COLLEGE BOYFRIEND.

I was 25 when I got diagnosed with endometriosis. All the trips to the emergency room, all the pain medications, birth control variations, anti-depressants, started to connect and give some type of meaning to my pain. I was 17 a few months away from going off to college when I had to go to the emergency room because my insides literally felt like they were about to prolapse out of my body. I was given no comfort there. I was basically told I may want to stop being "sexually active" because it is causing me pain. Listen you "unstable creature", I'm not "sexually active", I don't have any sexually transmitted diseases, I am only 17 and in pain! I don't know what labor feels like but on your scale of 1-10 mark it as 20! Again, victimized by the unknown. The years in between become grim. I was faced with surgeries, unemployment, death, car repossessions, theft. I even had to give up my apartment to move back with my parents because I couldn't make ends meet. I felt lower than low.

Disability may have saved me just a bit but not enough to survive. Now a victim to the once-a-month system.

Victim to Victor

All those years of pain, hurt, shame, guilt, silence, and heartache took pieces of me that I can never get

back! Now, I look back I was just a girl who at the time was told living check to check was "LIFE" and you just must accept it! A girl who grew up not talking about feelings and being victimized with words such as "I'll kill you if you tell" or "no one will believe you". I was silenced and as I grew into a woman my voice was no more. The voice and power the creator birthed in me was taken unwillingly. They were WRONG though! I'm still alive and well. My voice is finally being heard and that right there literally makes my heart smile and if that is what joy feels like, then I want more
of it.
The independence I gained from having to work and go to school at the age of 14 to having a vision at 17 that an entrepreneurial life will by milk and honey. Even while obtaining a college degree for something I could have taught myself and furthering my education when I what I really wanted to do was escape and travel the world. Do you hear me though?   I'm a w-o-m-a-n NOW, Entrepreneur &

Travel Professional, among other gifts & talents unforeseen. I know what it feels like when your faith is low nowhere else to turn, to ease the pain, you try to slit your wrist due to the highs and lows in LIFE! See, the difference between now and then is I dwell in my faith, as well as personal & self-development to grow. The creator didn't bring me this far to be silenced. My belief is on another level and each day I empower myself and others I connect with to conquer the small things to reach the ultimate goal. I no longer ask for permission BUT give notice that increase is in EVERY area of our life! I continue to find the treasure within, after all
"FROM WHERE YOUR HEART WANTS TO GO, YOU WILL FIND YOUR TREASURE"
and rise...

Entrepreneur & Travel Professional Alecia Tameko www.treasureprises.com info@treasureprises.com

10
TONSHAY THERESA
HAPPILY, EVER AFTER

A good Fairytale always ends with,

"They Lived Happily Ever After." The fairytale books always include a prince charming, a

fairytale castle and ends with a perfect life. As little girls, we are constantly exposed to this dream of what the perfect life is supposed to be. You prepare yourself your entire life for prince charming. You finally meet him. He wines and dines you, treats you like a princess, and finally asks the big question. Will you marry me? Of course, you say yes and start planning the wedding of your dreams. After your dream wedding, you buy your dream home. Now it's time to have some kids and live Happily Ever After.

The reality is not all women are going to have the Happily Ever After drafted up in Fairytales. If you are one of these women; what will life be like for you? If you don't get the perfect man, perfect house, and perfect life; will you still be happy? Do you truly need the Fairytale? What if the life you have created for yourself becomes your Happily Ever After?

I met my first prince charming in high school. He was everything that prince charming was supposed to be. He was handsome, he was nice, he had money, and treated me like a princess. He truly spoiled me and there was nothing I could ask for that he would not do. Just like he was my prince charming, I later found out that he was prince charming to several other women too. I remember, one of the girls walking up to the car very hysterical. I had no idea what was happening and when I finally realized she was hysterical because he was dating her to, my heart was crushed.

He tried everything to get me back and finally figured out how. He won me back with the magic words, Will You Marry Me? As I think back, I'm not sure what made me marry his lying cheating ass. Maybe, it was the game of winning. As I thought to myself, Ha Ha I won Bitches. The joke was on me. Marrying him was the first mistake of a long line of mistakes I would make pursuing my Fairytale and Happy Ever After.

After that fiasco, it was very hard for me to commit in a relationship. I was fine with dating but every time someone started talking about marriage I would run for the hills. It became a joke amongst me and my friends for a long time. Although we were joking about it, I still had to look deeper to figure out why I was so scared of marriage. After years of soul searching, I realized that I did not want to give up me to please someone else. Eventually I married again and that also was a big mistake. The second husband could not put his mother, baby mother, daughter or so-called females' friends in their place.

After almost 2 years of marriage, I packed up moved out and have not thought about looking back. It was the opposite feeling with him. It was more like y'all can have him I'm done.

THE REALITY IS NOT ALL WOMEN ARE GOING TO HAVE THE HAPPILY EVER AFTER DRAFTED UP IN FAIRYTALES. IF YOU ARE ONE OF THESE WOMEN; WHAT WILL LIFE BE LIKE FOR YOU? IF YOU DON'T GET THE PERFECT MAN, PERFECT HOUSE, AND PERFECT LIFE; WILL YOU STILL BE HAPPY? DO YOU TRULY NEED THE FAIRYTALE? WHAT IF THE LIFE YOU HAVE CREATED FOR YOURSELF BECOMES? YOUR HAPPILY EVER AFTER?

All my life all I ever wanted was to be HAPPY. I often wonder if it was my dream to get married and have kids or was that everyone else's dream for me. I really can't remember ever wanting kids. I love my child to death, but I don't ever remember thinking I am going to be a great mom or wanting lots of kids.

My son is the only person I have ever loved unconditionally. Maybe my son will be my one true great love story. I've never been willing to sacrifice for anyone but him. Maybe he will be the only part of the Fairytale that I will have. Is having parts of the Fairytale so bad? I know a lot of women that hang onto Fairytales. I have a close friend that has a husband who is a disrespectful cheater. All her family and friends know he cheats, and everyone talks about it but just not to her. If u met my friend, you would never know that any of this was going on. You would swear she was a happily married woman with this perfect life. She has a big, beautiful diamond ring, they own a nice home in a great neighborhood, they have several luxury cars, go on great vacations together and are great parents. Sometimes when I am at her home, I feel like I'm in a soap opera. There was an instance where her husband's mistress was at a bar-be-cue at their home pretending she was there with one of his friends. While attending this event I thought to myself, everyone playing in this scenario should win an Oscar Award.

I wonder if all the pretending and carrying all that emotional baggage is worth it. She is gaining tons of weight and always in and out the hospital for health reasons. During a recent surgery, the mistress sent a couple of us a picture through Facebook Messenger of him sleep in the bed with the caption, "I don't think he is making it to the hospital tonight." I went back and forth in my mind about saying something but choose not to. I knew she would stop talking to me before she would leave him. My friend is okay with her Happily Ever After consisting of a cheating husband and a whole bunch of material things and who am I to ruin that for her? Could her life be her Happily Ever After? Why not, if it makes her HAPPY.

I had a conversation with a lady I sat next to on an airplane. As we laughed about our careers and the possibility of never having a husband because of our work travels; She told me her story. It all started with a crush she had on a guy in her early twenties, but they never dated. They lost contact and reconnected later in life while she was in her late 30's. Everything moved quickly. Shortly after dating him, he convinced her and her child to move into his house. After living together for a short while he proposed, and they got married. She thought she had everything she ever wanted but things went bad quickly especially after she lost her job. Now that he had total control over her, his demeanor towards her changed from bad to emotionally and verbally abusive. She is a very headstrong individual, so his abusive behavior only motivated her to gain control of her life. After being unemployed for 6 months she found her dream job and was moving up the ranks pretty quickly at work. As a final act of trying to keep control, her husband mental and emotionally abusive became physical when he raped her as she was getting ready for work. Her Fairytale had just become her nightmare. She left for work that day with her child and they never returned.

She says she should have left when the verbal abuse began but she was holding on to a Fairytale that has left her scarred for life. She did not want the stigma again of being an unwed single mother so she stayed in the marriage longer than she should have. Now here is this beautiful woman full of life who never wants to get married again because her ex-husband ruined her Fairytale. I would have never guessed that this would be her story. She is single, living in 2 different countries, and enjoying life. She had just vacationed for 3 weeks in the Maldives. Could her awesome life be her Happily Ever After? Is the life she has now bad for a Happily Ever After? Why not, at least she is
HAPPY.

One of my closest friends is a powerhouse in Corporate America. She is a beautiful woman, very well educated, owns a luxury home, makes six figures, and drives a luxury vehicle. She has no children or husband, but she has accomplished everything she has set out to do in her life. She is an amazing daughter, sister, niece, aunt, and friend. She is everything that a fantastic woman is supposed to be. She has never let the things that she does not have keep her from living her best possible life.

It really bothers me that when I talk about her, the first thing people always ask is if she married or does she have kids. It also bothers me that people give her grief about not being married or having kids. Will not having kids or a husband keep her from having a Happily Ever After? Why can't having everything she wanted in life be good enough for her Happily Ever After? Why not, after all, she is Happy. What most people pretend not to know is marriage does not change the characteristics of a person. A liar will still be a liar, a cheater will still be a cheater, a go getter will still be a go getter. Marriage will bring out the best in some people and the worst in others. I can deal with hard times, but I don't deal with disrespect. In every relationship I always say," I can argue with you about something different every day, but I can't argue with you about the same thing every day" but I never saw daily arguing in my Fairytale. After over 20 years of dating and marriage combined, I can't say I have met anyone where we both wanted the same Happily Ever After. I have never loved anyone enough to give up my Happily Ever After for their Fairytale. I have never loved anyone enough to have another baby. I have never loved anyone enough to give up my vacations. I have not met anyone that makes me want to put my dreams on hold. I have my own ambitions outside of my relationship and I work toward them whether the man in my life likes it or not. I don't want to give up my Fairytale to help someone else achieve theirs. The right person for will fit into my Happily Ever After and I will fit in his.

    Another thing I realized was my so-called

Fairytale experiences did not make me happy. I am happier today being single than I was being married. I enjoyed raising my son a single mom with a great support system more than being a miserable married couple. I am happy living in my small apartment then in a big house hoping that every time something breaks a contractor is not ripping me off. I rather travel the world alone than have a man with me complaining the whole time. I enjoy traveling for work even if it keeps me away from the ones I love. I am enjoying, my extravagant vacations, erasing items from my bucket list, attending fantastic events, and having great new experiences. Most importantly I am really Happy.

So, what if I never meet my prince charming. So, what if I don't have any more kids. So, what if I don't own a home. I still have a Happily Ever After without my life being a storybook Fairytale. My story book Happily Ever After can be whatever I want it to be so

I started writing my own story. It took me a long time but once I stopped looking for the Fairytale and started creating my own Fairytale doing all the thing, I love I became the happiest I have ever been. My life did become my Fairytale and I'm basking in the Happily, Ever After I have created for myself. Why can't my life be my Happily Ever After? I might not have the Fairytale but after all, I'm HAPPY.

www.TonShayTheresa.com
tonshaytheresa@gmail.com
Facebook @tonshaytheresa
Instagram @tonshaytheresa

11
TONI HENDERSON-MAYERS
DIVAS WIN RELATIONSHIPS

Period! If you cannot manage your relationships, you have failed to encompass the true essence of a diva. I know, I know you are saying to yourself that the dictionary states that a "diva" is a self-absorbed, selfish, temperamental woman who must have her own way. You are right to say so because that is the definition of the word "diva". However, in this text "diva" takes on a different meaning. In this book, the term "diva" refers to being a queen. Before you give me the side eye, consider that once the word "diva" meant "goddess". Later, the word meant an opera singer, a soloist and in modern culture a moody, hard to get along with leading lady or performer. Who wants that moniker attached to them? I don't!!! In most recent times, women label themselves as "divas" to express seeing themselves as queens and deserving the best in life; not demanding it, but commanding it by their "lady like ways", education, business acumen, inner and outer beauty and overall invaluable wisdom. Having established what a "diva" really is, divas win by maintaining great relationships. The trouble with the old model of "divahood" is that to be a diva you had to make others feel bad to make yourself feel good. It is a terrible business model that doesn't work or temporarily at best.

Although divas tend to win in many areas of their life, they tend to neglect their romances. There is an understanding that it takes work to get their businesses off the ground, and work to grow their money, and even raise their children but hesitate at the thought of working on their love life.

Divas win in their romantic relationships. If you are not winning, why not? If your answer is packed with everything the other person did wrong, you are missing a true opportunity to win in this area. No relationship fails because the other person did everything right and you did nothing wrong. Sure, the other person could be a complete jerk, criminal in fact, but there is always something we can point to and say we could have done better. Is it possible you may have done everything right in your relationship but the one thing you did do wrong was to pick an abuser? Owning your mistakes and forgiving yourself is a great step to winning in your relationships.

I spend my life teaching others how to determine the true character and intent of their love interest. In my book, "Wise Courtship: Before Relationship & Marriage Guide" I address the question; do you know who you are in a relationship with? If you know more about hair, makeup, shoes and nails or you don't know as much as you should about the person you are in a relationship with, get a copy of my book so you too can win in your romances.

Divas win in their family relationships. Family members are the only people we have not chosen to be in an intimate relationship with. Somehow, we must learn how to have a healthy relationship with each member. This is not to say we will not have disagreements, conflicts and tough times. There are times when relationships with our family members are so toxic we must separate ourselves to relate better with each other. In some cases, a relationship must be limited or severed. Winning in your family relationship or any relationship for that matter doesn't mean you tolerate abuse. Winning in relationships mean you know how to MAINTAIN them.

Maintenance takes work. You may need to work with, pray for, teach, spend time with, encourage or correct in a healthy relationship. There are times when you may have to cut off bad ones. It's all part of maintaining and balancing relationships and a true diva knows the difference. I developed an online family on Facebook for those who were without family or just want more people to love. We support one another, encourage each other and want you to win. You are welcome to connect with the Wise Courtship Family on Facebook and benefit from our loving family support system.

Divas win in their friendships. Friendships are an awesome way to invite selected people to share in your most intimate and private time. Some of us have friends we grew up with or developed along life's journey. However, you collect your friends, true divas know that friends are chosen and must speak positively into your life. That is not to say that a friend cannot disagree with you or tell you the truth about yourself (which you may not want to hear). Divas know that friends earn the right to speak into your life. Friends can be a blessing.

Great friends share many days of laughter and tears. If you are blessed with an incredible friend, a diva will cherish that relationship and do what she can to make sure it continues to be satisfying for all parties.

Could you use more true friends or just surround yourself with others who want positive people in their lives? I developed the Wise Courtship Chapters for that very reason. Our chapters are located in the US but I hope to have them around the world. We usually meet every other month. Some meetings include workshops or seminars with networking opportunities and other meetups include a social event with networking. We have so much fun. It is an opportunity to meet and make other friends in your local area, in another state or during our annual conference. To find a chapter near you or start one, visit my website or email info@WiseCourtship.com for more information.

Divas definitely win in business. Unlike the stereotype of a diva who is temperamental, burns her bridges and is downright nasty, a diva knows that a great businesswoman develops her business relationships. In the era of reality shows, "The Apprentice" to name a few, many may believe being pushy, arrogant and rude is the way to do business. No one, including the bully, wants to work with a mean, nasty or forceful person. Great business begins with great relationships, the end result, great perpetual profits!

People like doing business with people they like. Of course, you may do business with someone you don't care much for, but when you have a choice you will choose to do business with someone you get along with. At some point, a colleague will have a choice of who to do business with and you want that choice to be you.

Divas know that every customer, colleague or even competitor is important, and collaborations can keep her on the cutting edge. A diva is a builder and not a bridge burner. She builds businesses or creates streams of income. She doesn't wait until she is accepted into circles but creatively builds her own. I realize many would love to be able to start a business, build their own platform or create streams of income but are not sure how. I created the Wise Courtship Prosperity Club for that reason. Membership in this club helps each person grow prosperous with every click. The monthly training alone is so worth the membership but of course, you receive so much more. Check out each membership level and the benefits at bit.ly/JoinWCPC. The link is case sensitive so be sure to add the exact link in your web browser.

Divas have a wonderful relationship with themselves. She knows what she says to herself is so important. It is essential that she deals with her "baggage" and "issues" so her most appealing qualities will be able to shine through. Harboring grudges and ill will causes a diva to age quickly. There is nothing wrong with aging, but one should do so beautifully and gracefully. It is nearly impossible to find a woman who keeps her beauty while being hateful, callus and unforgiving. This type of attitude begins to eat away at you like cancer and poisons everything you touch or connect with. It is a silent and total killer.

If you are dealing with past hurts, deal with them today. Forgiveness doesn't give a pass to the person who hurt you. It simply helps you to release the power the person has over you, cleanse your body from the toxic mess that's trapped inside of you so that love and light can flow in. Each morning I broadcast on Periscope as @WiseCourtship to help listeners take a closer look at self so that they can enjoy other relationships in their life. Do not be stuck in a toxic situation that can overtake their life. I also broadcast on radio, Facebook Live, and YouTube at bit.ly/ToniTube. If you need to get your self-relationship on track, be sure to check me out. Divas realize their ultimate strength comes from someone other than themselves. There are times when you just don't know how you will make it. There are times when you may feel like giving up. Sometimes you don't know what to do. In my opinion, a wise diva learns to pray and turn to God. Of course, not everyone believes in the Almighty, but I have found God to be an essential part of my life. When I pray, I receive clarity and direction? God speaks to me. His voice is not audible (although it certainly can be) but He makes small suggestions, sometimes so quiet and subtle that if I am not careful to listen closely, I would miss it.

Praying helps a diva know that she is not alone and that she has someone she can talk to and release her innermost thoughts without fear of being revealed. In my darkest hour prayer helped me to get through it. When I wasn't sure of my next move in life, prayer helped me see the next path I should follow. When I had doubts, I could win, prayer settled my fears. Every Sunday at 3:00 pm EST, I pray for people's concerns and give a word of encouragement on my Facebook page. Prayer changes things. I believe in it so much. I pray weekly for those who choose to be prayed for.

Divas have a great relationship with their money. This is one relationship where you can totally tell the other party what to do. In the case of money, having a budget is telling your money what to do. Some of us are chasing our money, begging our money to come back. Others see their money cheating on them by being in another's pockets or riding in a fancy car or living in a beautiful home. Their money seems to be with everyone else but with them.

A diva knows she needs to get a handle on her money. Are you in debt? How much debt do you have? What is your credit score? What do you do when you want to raise your credit score? What is an asset? What is a liability? How many assets do you have? What are your investments? How long can you live without a job? Are you able to answer these questions? with favorable answers? Divas can provide for themselves. When she decides to marry, she can combine incomes and win even more. She can win for herself but also for her whole family. Her ability to handle money well is passed down to her children and taught to those around her. If you feel you need to grow in this area, consider my coaching sessions and upcoming courses in debt elimination, credit repair and creating streams of income. Join my newsletter on my website to stay abreast of all upcoming courses and coaching sessions. bit.ly/EraseDebtCreateStreams

Divas win by being wise with their time and build a better life for themselves, their family and community each day.

My Wins –

Toni Henderson-Mayers a sought-after

TV/Radio Relationship Expert, Author/Speaker whose message encourages us all to find relationships we are "excited about" and to look for passion in our lives.

Toni is the CEO and Founder of Word Therapy Publishing, LLC., which publishes books, audio, and video to encourage, empower and heal audiences. She is also the owner of Alphabet Theater Workshop, which performs dramatic readings of almost anything from children's stories to The Bible. You can also see Toni on stage or in various films or TV commercials.

Toni was the past radio personality for 91.9 FM, WNTI and AM 1430, WNJR, New Jersey and currently, hosts "The Job Alternative" podcast and "Wise Courtship" which is accessible on iTunes or her website. Most recently Toni joined the STELLAR AWARD WINNING All Nations Radio Network with her own show, The Wise Courtship Philosophy Show.

Toni Henderson-Mayers is the co-author of "One Great Idea", which is a collaboration with other successful business colleagues on various business ideas. Her book, "Wise Courtship: Before Relationship & Marriage Guide" has earned worldwide distribution and audience and a nomination for a Shelf Award. Wise Courtship help seal her title of TV/Radio Expert as she was heard on over a hundred stations in one year. She is also a contributing writer to the book, "Share & Grow Rich" and "Hiring Now" magazine.

In 2017, Toni launched the Wise Courtship Prosperity Club designed to help others start a business, build their own platform and create streams of income. In 2018 her Wise Courtship Chapters launched in 6 locations and 5 states created for people to locally meet up to network, learn, attend social events, collaborate and more.

Recently Toni was awarded The People's Choice Award at the ACHI Magazine Awards for exceptional work and inspiration she brings to thousands globally and was a finalist for the Indie Author Legacy Award (IALA) for her book Wise Courtship in the category of Relationships. Also, Toni helps launch two-time Emmy nominated Never Settle Show as Crowd Producer. Toni is married to actor and playwright, Brian McClure Mayers and has two sons.

Winning Point – Divas win by cultivating relationships. If the relationship isn't working, move on. If the relationship is a winner, cherish and take care of it.

12
LESLIE EPPS

Darkness, the opposite to brightness, is understood as a lack of visible light. This can also apply to everyday life. I spotted a friend one day while crossing the street on my way home from working at the apartment complex where I also lived. She was a bus driver and was passing by as I was crossing. The look on her face was pure disbelief. At the time I didn't know what that look meant. Later that evening I received a phone call from her asking me if I was ok. That was the start of my healing.

I had been feeling detached from the world for quite some time and had reached a point where I would only go to work and back home. Never leaving my neighborhood. The feeling that something was missing in my life was overwhelming and nothing I did felt complete. I had begun to lose a tremendous amount of weight and people had started to treat me very mean as if they had no respect for me. A few people even called me a "crackhead" but that was not the case. I found myself constantly arguing with people and defending myself on a regular. Bottom line is I didn't realize how much weight I had really lost, and that people will assume what they want about you spread rumors while trying to treat you as such. There were moments that I would sit in my apartment and cry. I was completely fed up so, I prayed and asked God to remove anything and anyone from my life that was causing me pain. Then, after several nights of waking up around 3 a.m. God spoke to my spirit and told me it was time for me to move. It was so clear I answered whispering "Where am I supposed to go". Then I thought to myself anywhere would be better than here If I ever want to stop feeling the way that I was feeling. Within a month I had quit my job, packed all my belongings, and moved out of my apartment. I didn't even have another job lined up, but I made that move strictly on faith and wanting a better life. I had decided that once I prayed and God gave me that message, it was time to sit in the back of the limo and let God lead me from that point on. I soon found out that moving from that apartment was only the beginning of my journey. And I'm here to tell you, I got just what I asked for. A "friend" of mines that knew my situation opened her home to me. I happily accepted and was so appreciative. I had started to feel a lot better about removing myself from that depressing place and within 1 week I found another job. It didn't take me long to realize that you really don't know people until you live with them. Watch who you confide in and who you accept help from. when a person with a low self-esteem offers their help, control will play a big part in that situation.

    If you're still feeling down, everything is fine. As soon as you start to feel better and your situation starts to change for the better things start to get ugly. Some people want to use your dark times to make themselves feel better. So, after a couple of months, I moved again. I left there going to another "friends" house. That move was a little worse than the first. Control is a very mild word to describe that experience. But I refused to be treated any kind of way just because someone was helping me. Another FRIEND (the bus driver) insisted that I stop trusting all these so-called concerned people that wanted to use me as their punching bag. She told me to pack my belongings and come to her house. That was where I had the most peace. I only stayed short term but I started to realize who my real friends were and that I went to those other places so part of my prayers could be answered. I asked God to remove those people from my life and he did.

As soon as you start to feel better and your situation starts to change for the better things start to get ugly. Some people want to use your dark times to make themselves feel better.

Another long-time FRIEND called me and was telling me that her mom had moved out of her house and they were looking for a tenant. I moved there two days later. Everything was starting to get better. I enjoyed my job, my daughter came to live with me, and I had started to feel like my old self. I still felt like something was missing Georgia is somewhere that I've always wanted to move to and for years my friends and family tried to convince me to move there. It was 3 A.M. and once again I woke up again with another message from God saying it's time to move. That's when I realized It was time for me to leave Gary. From the beginning that's the move God was trying to tell me. I came across a male from my past who lives in Mississippi. He suggested that I move there. At this point, my whole attitude has changed, and I was very cautious although I knew It was time for me to go. When God speaks so clearly to my spirit. I rely solely on my faith no matter what my current situation. Before I left several people tried to convince me not to go. Coincidentally my job lost their contract, I picked up my last paycheck and the next day I headed to Mississippi. As soon as my first foot touched Mississippi ground, God spoke again and said this isn't it either. I laughed because I immediately knew I was out of there the first chance I got. It was also felt good that I had no worries despite everything. That's how I knew I was on the right track. 1 ½ months later, I was MOVING to Georgia and that was the best MOVE of my life.

It was somewhat of a struggle at first, but I am happy now and have been since I arrived. 1 year and 2 months later I now have multiple incomes and am about to start my own business. Bottom line recognize who your true friends are and remove yourself from toxic relationships. Sometimes people will see how great you are but use your downfall to try and tear you down, know that your situation does not define who you are. Stay joyful no matter what. When you speak to God and he starts to speak back, pay close attention and you'll know when you're on the right track.

My limo ride led me into the light, and I feel Great.
Leslie Epps
Les Create

13
SHONDA ORLICIA FAITH,SACRIFICE +VICTORY

"Faith is the substance of thing hoped for and the evidence of things not seen." (Hebrews 11:1) As I look back, I realized that faith has brought me a very long way in my life. I grew up on the west side of Chicago a place where not many people make it out of. My mother passed away when I was about 6 months, I was raised by my grandmother who adopted me. My family lived in a 3-story apartment building owned by my grandmother. I guess you can see why "Faith" fits perfectly into the equation, growing up faith was all we had. My mother was a strong and independent woman. While Pastoring a church she was still able to raise me and my siblings and keep the house in order. As I got older, I watched my mom and often asked how she made things possible for us to have, she would always say to me "by faith". She would pray and ask God to see us through daily.

    My mother didn't have the funds to get me the things everyone else had but she made sure I never looked a mess. In high school, I was always called "Ms. quite" or "Church girl" because I was a preacher's kid. As I got older, I started "smelling myself" my mother would say, I never disrespected her though. Talking to boys was my mother's main concern. I had one boy that I brought to the house. She spoke briefly with him about his intentions with me, he answered "we're just friends' "and that's all he was. My life suddenly changed when I fell in love and got pregnant with my first child. When I found out I was pregnant I was so scared to tell mom because I was only 16 going on 17. She already assured me we were going to get through this together, "but once you have this baby, I'm going to tear your behind up "I can still hear her shouting at me.

Being a young mother was hard but with my mother's help and God on our side I was able to have a healthy baby boy. After I had my son my mother explained to me my life is not my own anymore, I have someone that is going to need me every single day. It was time for me to grow up. Immediately my mother started to show me the true meaning of patience and understanding faith. A couple of years later I had my second child, at this point in my life, I didn't have my mother anymore, she became ill. I did what I had to do as a parent and found a job at the corner restaurant. I lied about my age so I could provide for my family. It was me, my mother and my two babies. My life was never the same as when my mother died. That was one of the worse days of my life. Unbelievable, I went from having my mother as my backbone and my everything to being all alone with my babies. I never experienced this kind of pain and hurt before. I remember sitting in the house asking God what am I going to do? Once my mom passed no one was there it was just me and my babies. The day of the funeral I was dressing my children and I heard a voice say, "I'm with you always sweetie, I will never leave you". At that moment, I knew I would be alright. After the funeral, I was all alone again no one called to check on me and my kids, but it was ok I knew I had more responsibilities to be concerned about. The next day my grandfather came to the house and said I need to talk to you. I said yes sir, he said boo you can't stay in this house it is not safe. I told him it has been safe for me for 20 years I can't leave, he said you can't stay because they are about to shut off all the utilities. I started crying and said I can't leave mom she comes and see about us he said baby mom is gone you will see her again one day, but you can't stay. So, I packed up the kids and went and stayed with my grandfather. On the way to his house, he said you know you have more family. I said yes, I know, he said no, you have other family members you have not met yet. When we got to his house all I remember was this lady staring at me. I knew everyone else in the house but her, so I said hello. She looked at me and said Lord, that is my sister child. I had no idea what she was talking about because remember I lost my birth mom at six months and just lost my grandmother. At this point I'm all confused. This lady had big hair and sipping on a Pepsi, with a Kool 100 cigarette in her hand. She said do you know who I am? I said no ma'am, she said I'm your aunt. She went on telling me these stories about my birth mom and my birthday and I'm looking at her like, lady you sure you got the right kid. She looks at me and said I know it's a lot but now that we found you, I'm not going to lose you. I started spending time with her and had a chance to meet my cousins. Then she told me that It was time to meet my father. I looked at her and asked, My father? He's still alive? Because I was told something else. She said, girl your daddy stays on the south side. Once again

in my head I'm saying this is too much for me. One day my aunt planned a get together this is where I met more aunts and cousins. I found out one of my cousins was my sister. Yes, I said my cousin is my sister. My life seemed to be this crazy maze that I could not seem to figure out on my own. I only found myself going in circles trying to map out all the missing pieces. Out of all my silly mistakes, struggles and sacrifices I would never regret everything I've been through. God has seen me through so much I would be writing for days if I listed everything in this chapter. I encourage all people to turn your life over to God and he will truly open the heavens to you. See, many times we are so focused on the circumstances that we forget "this too shall pass". I can clearly look back now and say everything the enemy meant to destroy me God has made for my good. Even though I thought I would never make it out of a spiral circle life of bad choices, drowning in debt and poverty, I can stand tall and proud and say, "But God". Regardless of what you see, God has plans for you that you could never imagine.

> I can clearly look back now and say everything the enemy meant to destroy me God has made for my good.

I know who I am and whose I am. I am the daughter of an awesome God. Jesus died on the cross for little oh me so that I could be amazing. You can have the same. All you must do is accepted Jesus Christ into your life and allow him to lead and guide you to the life he created for you.

I WAS WINNING WHEN I DIDN'T EVEN KNOW IT

I accepted Christ when I was 10 years old in 1987. Once I was done with my own plan and began to follow God's plan for my life. Then and only then, I was able to accomplish things attached to my purpose.

- ✓ In 2011, I received my Associates Degree in Medical Science.
- ✓ In 2012 I received my ministry License to Teach Liturgical Dance with The Eagle Institute of Dance
- ✓ In 2014 because of some health challenges, I was not able to work and was forced to leave my job. My God is so awesome because this life event somehow ushered me into my current business, my Travel Company.
- ✓ In June 2016 I relocated from Chicago to Atlanta and became a homeowner.
- ✓ In August 2017, I became a wife to my amazing husband.
- ✓ My children are all grown now. My husband and I are grandparents of 2 and soon to be 3.

Continue to keep your faith strong in Jesus, do your part and you can't go wrong. I am much stronger, wiser and living life to my full potential. If God can do it for me, he can do it for you.

When I tell you, I have come through so many tough situations that God turned It around. In between I made major sacrifices to survive so my children could live a good life. It didn't matter how far the job I worked It. I had jobs that only allowed me to see my babies in bed. Some jobs I would leave home at 5am and wouldn't get home to them until 10 or 11pm at night. I had to trust babysitters that treated my babies wrong and I didn't know until I got home that my babies were treated badly. I worked many jobs from restaurants, retail, telemarketing, you name it I did it, all to make sure my babies were good. The bible says in Philippians 4:13, I can do all things through Christ that strengthens me. I can honestly say I didn't understand this verse until I started walking in my faith and my truth.

As a mother I really had to put things I wanted to do for myself aside yes, I wanted to go have fun, but my children came first. I wanted to finish college, but I had to work to make sure my kids were well taken care of. I can say my biggest sacrifice was missing a few years of my children's lives because I was raising them alone. I was mother, doctor, and daddy. I was all the above and trust me there were lots of nights I cried that I missed a day of them growing up. I asked God please, I need to see my babies they need me Lord I can't keep leaving them with people that will hurt them, they only have me. God heard me and he sent to me this beautiful woman that loved my children like her own. I was blessed with a job that did not require me to work on weekends and allowed me to be home to get them from the afterschool program. I was truly grateful, and I was also able to go back to school myself and get my college degree. And I did all of this as a single mom and not one time on drugs. It's the little things that mean sooooo much when I think back on my life. I pray my story can help someone who is going through in life. I made it as a single mom with four kids now married, a grandmother that raised her babies on faith, sacrifice and victory with the help of God (Jesus Christ).

14
APRIL DELILLY
SHOTS FIRED…BUT I'M STILL BULLET PROOF

"Pow"! was the sound I heard and kept hearing in my head for years after my husband of 19 ½ years decided to put a bullet in his head while sitting on our living room couch during the time which me, my mother and 3 of our 4 children were home on April 23, 2010. I was distraught, devastated, depressed, confused and very angry! My whole life changed in an instant and there was nothing I could do about it.

Having grown up in the church, I knew God could help me through this, but I was harboring unforgiveness in my heart towards my husband and I wasn't ready to let it go. Besides, I had a right to be angry, right? Wrong! But it would take me some time to realize it.

Thank God I had a very strong support system of family and friends who continuously prayed for us because now, I was out there doing whatever I wanted to do and didn't care who didn't like it...including my children. I dated, partied, drank and traveled. I bought my children cars and material things, but I wasn't establishing a new relationship with them. I didn't realize they were angry too! But can you believe they weren't angry with him? They were angry with me! What? Why? I didn't leave or kill myself...I'm still here! Why on earth are they mad at me? I discovered my children were angry with me because they felt like I didn't care. They were used to spending quality time with their dad and us doing family-oriented things and now they were left with their mom who was out there "wilding out". I was there for them physically and financially, but not emotionally. That's where I messed up. I was more concerned about what he did to "me" and not what he did to "us". Once I got some things out of my system, I realized my anger towards him had stopped me from grieving and placed a wedge between me and my children which prevented us from bonding and building a new relationship. I could not continue this way, or I could lose my children too, and that was not an option. Grieving is an important process to overcome the loss of a loved, one and when we don't allow ourselves to grieve, there could be serious consequences that can and will affect your future. Once I allowed myself to grieve, I was finally able to forgive him. The feeling of abandonment lifted. I felt free, my mind was clear, and I was able to accept the fact that it was "his" decision. That's what "he" wanted and now I had to put on my big girl panties and move on.

Six months later, I moved on to the next chapter in my life. I started online dating. I met a lot of nice gentlemen, but I didn't want a relationship. I wanted to have fun and have great sex with no strings attached. I was living foul by dating married men too. I was enjoying my new-found freedom, meeting new people and experiencing life like I should've done in my 20's, but I was married with children. Being single started to get old to me. I wasn't cut out for this. I missed the family lifestyle. I missed all the "small" things we take for granted in a marriage. I had now experienced both the married and single lifestyles and realized I wanted to be a wife again! I'm selfish! I didn't want to share! I wanted to have my OWN man who was committed to loving only me! The Bible says, "he who finds a wife...", so my interpretation of that scripture was that I should not be looking for a man, he should be looking for me. I logged into my online account, so I could hide my profile. While doing so, I had messages in my inbox. I read the messages from several gentlemen, but only 1 stood out. This was the 2nd message I received from him that I had not read. The message included his telephone number, so I wrote it down, read his profile, and viewed his pictures. He didn't look too bad based off the photos. Lol. After talking on the phone for a little more than a week, we met in person on July 27, 2013 and from then on, it was on and popping! Our 1st date was a weekend together. Yes, I spent the whole weekend with him! Don't judge me, I'm grown! Lol, Needless to say, we were inseparable and married on June 13, 2014. We had a beautiful wedding, reception and honeymoon and now our life together as one has begun. My husband is a professional truck driver and owns a photography business. He always dreamed of having his wife in the truck with him, so what did I do? I went to truck driving school in November 2014 and got my Class A CDL so I could help make his dreams come true. OMG! This was so fun! We were now working and playing together. Yes, we had our disagreements, but not that often. People would ask us how we could be together every day all day. It was easy because we are friends, and we respect each other's space. Life was good! We were vacationing at least 2 times a year, taking weekend getaways, enjoying couple events and making money with our photography business. Around November 2016, we began making plans to relocate to Arizona and trying to decide how we would go about starting our truck driving school. Our future was bright. We were now on one accord! Our marriage vows said for better or worse, in sickness and in health. Boy oh boy was my husband tested on the "in sickness and in health" vow because on July 10, 2017, I was admitted to the hospital and eventually told I had Non-Hodgkin's T-Cell Lymphoma which is a blood cancer. Wow! My world was turned upside down AGAIN! I was afraid that it would be too much for my husband and he would leave. I was afraid that I would die of this cancer like my only sister did in December 2011 at the age of 40. After sharing my fears with my husband, he assured me that the thought of leaving me NEVER crossed his mind. He said he took our wedding vows to heart. The timing of this news couldn't have been worse! We had our grandchildren with us for the summer, we had just taken in our 3 nieces and 1 of them was 6 months pregnant!

But God!

The doctors were working hard to find a way to save me. I could no longer walk, could barely talk, had urine and bowel catheters and a feeding tube.

They told me and my husband I was dying!

Wow! My world was turned upside down AGAIN! I was afraid that it would be too much for my husband and he would leave. I was afraid that I would die of this cancer like my only sister did in December 2011 at the age of 40.

They were doing test after test, trying all kinds of medicines and I was growing weary. I had been praying and wondering why God hadn't healed me.

I knew He could, but I was tired of them sticking me, taking my blood, giving me blood transfusions, CT scans and ultrasounds of everybody part. The chemo treatments were taking a toll on me. I lost my hair, my skin turned very dark and I lost over 80 pounds. I was weak and getting depressed. I would look in the mirror and cry because I didn't recognize the woman I was looking at. She was ugly to me. I thank God for my awesome support system who prayed for me daily! My husband would not wait for the nurse to clean me up after I had a bowel movement, he did it! He would go on the road on Sunday, come back on Friday and spend the weekend at the hospital with me. Wow! What a man! My dad flew in from California for a week and my mom was there often praying and making sure no negativity was spoke around me. My daughter drove me to chemo and to doctor's appointments. I was in the hospital and rehabilitation center for over 3 months, and I had visitors EVERY DAY! My family, church and friends were VERY supportive! The devil tried to make me lose my mind and kill me, but it didn't work! As of January 2018, I'm in remission…cancer FREE! God has me here for a purpose. I'm a work in progress and each day I get stronger and stronger. I am slowly embracing the "new" me and thanking God I'm alive! I survived the pain of suicide, was blessed with another great husband and I beat cancer! I'm victorious thanks to God! In the words of Destiny's Child, "I'm a survivor, I'm not gone give up, I'm not gone stop, I'm gone work harder, I'm a survivor, I'm going to make it, I will survive, Keep on surviving"!

Be Blessed

CONNECT WITH
REAL DIVAS WIN
WWW.REALDIVASWIN.COM

JOIN US IN FUTURE RDW ANTHOLOGIES AND RELEASE YOUR STORY, BUILD WEALTH AND YOUR CREDIBILITY AS AN AUTHOR

WWW.REALDIVASWINANTHOLOGY
**FOLLOW US ON SOCIAL MEDIA
@REALDIVASWIN**
TWITTER. FACEBOOK. INSTAGRAM

www.ingramcontent.com/pod-product-compliance
Lightning Source LLC
Chambersburg PA
CBHW071417070526
44578CB00003B/592